C000015825

UNION

THE HEART OF RUGBY

UNION

THE HEART OF RUGBY

PAUL THOMAS

with

MARTIN JOHNSON — JOHN KIRWAN — JOEL STRANSKY

NICK FARR-JONES — PHILIPPE SELLA

PHOTO EDITORS: KELSEN BUTLER AND GEOFF BLACKWELL

VSP

in association with PQ Blackwell

PRIDE
HONOUR
PASSION
PAIN

TEAM
COURAGE
HEROES
GLORY

"What I really love about rugby, what will remain with me forever, is that thing of creating strong bonds on the pitch, that will go on off it, for the rest of my life."

ALESSANDRO TRONCON

Heroes motivate fans to get up in the middle of the night to watch a rugby match 20 time zones away.

Heroes send kids outside to chase a rugby ball around and make promising young players vow that one day they too will wear the jersey.

Heroes inspire their team-mates to get off their knees when their bodies scream for relief and to be better players than they thought they were.

HEROES

Heroes instil the love of the game that is rugby's heartbeat.

Heroes don't contemplate failure. Some shy away from taking responsibility; heroes revel in it. Some see the risk of letting the team down; heroes see an opportunity to seize the initiative.

Heroes instil the love of the game that is rugby's heartbeat.

We have five heroes to guide us on our rugby journey.

Nick Farr-Jones was an outstanding all-round sportsman at Sydney's Newington College but wasn't considered a good enough rugby player for the first XV. In 1984, he was plucked from the obscurity of second-division club rugby and then, in quick succession, was selected for Sydney, Australian Universities and the Wallaby team to tour the UK. He made his test debut against England at Twickenham in what proved to be the first leg of a Grand Slam.

In 1988, Bob Dwyer became Wallaby coach for the second time, having been dumped four years earlier. According to legend, he began the first training run of his second coming thus: "As I was saying before I was so rudely interrupted..." One of his first acts was to hand the captaincy to 25-year-old Farr-Jones.

The new regime didn't have overnight success but in 1990 the Wallabies issued a warning to the world by defeating the All Blacks at Athletic Park, Wellington, ending a four-year, 23-game winning streak. A local newspaper commented: "The great captains, the great halfbacks have vision, and that's what Farr-Jones displayed in the Wellington wind and rain. He saw the ground as a chessboard."

The following year brought the ultimate glory. In the dying seconds of the World Cup final, with Australia ahead but England still able to send the game into extra time with a converted try, Dwyer leapt to his feet and howled: "Kick it to the shithouse!" Observers couldn't tell whether the Queen, sitting a few feet away, was amused or not.

A UK rugby magazine said the Wallabies' victory "proves conclusively that nice guys can win".

In his autobiography, *A Life in Focus*, legendary New Zealand press photographer Peter Bush, who had been covering the All Blacks for decades, recalled an encounter with Farr-Jones and his team-mates Michael Lynagh and David Campese on the eve of the Australia–New Zealand semifinal in Dublin: "They were going out for a meal, would [my partner and I] like to join them? I thought, am I hearing this right? So we had a couple of drinks and a meal. I said I thought they'd be tucked up in bed but as far as they were concerned it was just a normal night."

"At one point, Lynagh and Farr-Jones were fine-tuning a double-round move using the salt and pepper shakers. I said: 'Maybe we should sit at another table.' 'Don't be silly, mate,' they said. 'We've got nothing to hide.' It was so refreshing to see that, despite the importance of the occasion, these guys hadn't lost sight of the fact that it was just a game of rugby. In contrast to their affability, the All Blacks were rather taciturn and stand-offish and, whereas the Aussies were still tinkering and innovating at the eleventh hour, there was an air of arrogance about the All Blacks, as if all they had to do was turn up and the cup would be theirs once again – an assumption, I hasten to add, that I shared."

Since his retirement in 1993, Farr-Jones has had limited involvement with the game, although in 2010 he was appointed to the board of the New South Wales Rugby Union. Now he talks about the game as directly and incisively as he played it, offering blunt advice for those who aspire to follow in his footsteps:

"I've never been in a gym in my life. They wanted me to have a couple of sessions with a psychologist; I said: 'Get stuffed.' You could do that as an amateur. I believe over-analysis leads to paralysis; just let talented people go out there with the semblance of a game plan and strut their stuff and be spontaneous."

"The best players have the best work ethic but they are spontaneous. It's not about watching hours of video – let the coach do that. Beforehand, the coach can say we've identified four areas of weakness we think we can exploit and three strengths to watch out for. That's enough."

"I believe every test match is there to be won but what ends up on your rugby coffin is how you went at the World Cup. I don't think that's a bad thing – it's how you handle the pressure. Sometimes the nation imposes more pressure than you might want. It's about handling the pressure and making good judgement calls and, if you're not up to it, *c'est la vie*. Sometimes I think people should get day jobs and have to make a few more decisions in real life, rather than just having to make some big ones every four years and getting them wrong."

Heroes send kids outside to chase a rugby ball around and make promising young players vow that one day they too will wear the jersey.

Heroes motivate fans to get up in the middle of the night to watch a rugby match 20 time zones away.

One of the sharpest Kiwi-baiting taunts by British rugby writer Stephen Jones is that Colin Meads, generally regarded as the greatest All Black of them all, is actually the second-best lock forward to come out of the King Country province. The best, insists Jones, is England's Martin Johnson, who played for King Country during an 18-month stay in New Zealand in 1989/90.

While some Kiwi fans will bristle at anyone, let alone a Pom, being mentioned in the same breath as the great Pinetree, it's clear that this pair had more in common than locking the King Country scrum.

There's a striking – an apt word – similarity in tone and content between what Johnson says about his hard-man reputation in his autobiography ("Neanderthal. A glowering thug. The Terminator in shorts. And that's just my wife's opinion.") and similar passages in Alex Veysey's 1974 biography, *Colin Meads: All Black*.

"You either let a guy cannon into the back of you and take it, or you draw a line in the sand," says Johnson. "Rugby is a game of physical confrontation and you cannot afford to back down, even if you want to."

Meads made this comment on dropping pint-sized British Lions fly-half David Watkins with a crisp back-hander: "If anyone belts me, I belt back. When you react to that sort of provocation, you react urgently."

Like Meads, Johnson could take it as well as dish it out and he subscribed to a code that could be summarised as "never apologise, never complain". An opponent who posed for a press photographer displaying scars supposedly inflicted by Johnson earned this withering blast: "You've got a one-inch cut under your eye, for God's sake. You're a grown man and a professional rugby player, not a little old lady who's been beaten up on her doorstep."

Johnson's magnificent career – two Heineken Cups, five Six Nations championships, five English premiership titles, two Grand Slams, the only player to captain the British and Irish Lions twice – ended in fairy-tale fashion at the 2003 World Cup in Australia.

It's safe to assume Martin Johnson doesn't believe in fairy tales and isn't prey to romantic notions. Asked what was going through his head when a six-man England pack held the All Blacks' scrum at bay at Wellington in 2003, he replied: "My spine".

His view of England's World Cup triumph and his current role as England manager is not that of a man with an eye on his place in history, but that of a rugby warrior for whom the camaraderie and the contest are each their own reward.

"What you remember is getting there: the journey. Winning the World Cup is great but that's not what it's about. When we were wandering around the field after the final, it would have mattered half a per cent to me if we hadn't won because doing it is what it's all about."

"We just wanted to get the game played, win it and go home. But when you get back to normality and the family, you miss it. It's strange – when you're in the middle of it and you ask guys if they're enjoying themselves, enjoyment isn't necessarily the thing that comes to mind. That's because of the pressure – it's tough at times so you have mixed feelings. But it's addictive; nothing beats it so you miss it when it's gone. You take the risk that you can win and be a hero or lose and be a failure and suffer the disappointment, but that's sport and you have to have perspective."

Such is Johnson's talismanic status in English rugby that, in 2008, aged 38 and with no coaching experience, he was appointed manager of the national team. When an overnight transformation wasn't forthcoming, he found himself caught in a crossfire: on one side were those who scorned the notion that the great man's aura, personality and will power were a substitute for hands-on coaching experience; on the other were those who didn't want to see their heroe's reputation tarnished.

Could he understand where the latter were coming from?

"Absolutely, we've all done that. We want our heroes to have perfect endings, to go out on a high, unblemished by failure. As it is, you get put on an extraordinary pedestal; it's just unreal – you'd think I'd never lost a game. But what are you going to do – just stop? This is what I do."

Before Jonah Lomu, there was John Kirwan. Just as Lomu electrified a watching world in 1995, so Kirwan's extraordinary length-of-the-field try against Italy in the opening match of the inaugural World Cup swept away the considerable scepticism surrounding the tournament and trumpeted the arrival of a new global sporting event.

Heroes don't contemplate failure. Some shy away from taking responsibility; heroes revel in it. Some see the risk of letting the team down; heroes see an opportunity to seize the initiative.

Although Kirwan in full flight epitomised the power of the black machine, it was already clear that this was a very different kind of All Black – a man in many ways ahead of his time. He employed a personal trainer to design and implement a programme that would boost his speed and strength, making him a strike weapon even from his own goal-line. He took an interest in fashion, he had sharp commercial instincts, he was open to outside influences and indeed to the world. He was the prototype for the new-age rugby star with global reach.

Most revolutionary of all is that he bared his soul, revealing that there was a dark side – a deeply misunderstood one – to this apparently golden existence: he suffered from depression. The hero constantly wrestled with far more daunting opponents than any he had to confront on the rugby field.

In his autobiography, *Running on Instinct*, published when he was still playing international rugby, Kirwan wrote: "I've come to terms with it now. At first it fills you with such fear and dread that you panic. Once you know it and can recognise it and stop panicking, you can begin to handle it. Then it becomes a case of trying to get through the day without thinking about it. It's a little like getting over a broken heart; you know you're through it when you don't think about your lost love too often and, when you do, there isn't that stab of pain."

"Life isn't always a smooth ride; bad things are coming down all the time and sometimes they come down on you. When that happens you've got to endure, you've

got to make sure that you learn from it, and then you go forward armed with whatever knowledge can be salvaged from the experience."

Kirwan continues to front mental health and depression awareness campaigns in New Zealand and, in 2007, was awarded an MBE for his services to these causes.

These days he is a true citizen of the world, a multilingual New Zealander who commutes from his home near Venice to coach Japan. His intense involvement in the game – he coached Italy between 2002 and 2005 – has done nothing to dim his enthusiasm. As befits a man who seldom looks back, he takes issue with players from previous generations who insist it was better in their day.

"Was it fun being an All Black?" he says. "If you dropped a ball at training, you'd get shit. It was a hard-edged environment that wouldn't let you fail. If you couldn't handle it, you got spat out."

"I sometimes hear old players saying these guys today aren't as good as we were. I just look at them and ask: did you ever go to the gym? These guys are superb athletes and have the same friendship and bond. I just think it's a very different world. They have a lot more scrutiny and many more responsibilities and probably can't get up to the larrikin stuff that we did. Last year the All Blacks were in bed by ten o'clock after they'd played the Wallabies at Eden Park because they were flying to Africa at four in the morning. In our day the socialising would have just been warming up, so maybe they don't have as much fun as we did."

And he remains committed to his ideal of rugby as a game of courage and daring for players who are both stoic and imaginative, who embrace both the harsh physicality and the spirit of adventure inherent in a code played with ball in hand.

"The thing about rugby is that you can't do what they do in soccer – just pass the ball back to the keeper. You've got to go forward, you can't go backwards, and going forward often means running into big, tough men. And it's not just about winning the World Cup: whether the All Blacks win it or not, they'll still be the Brazil of rugby if they continue to play in that attacking style."

The bare facts of Philippe Sella's career almost speak for themselves: won 111 caps for France playing in every Five Nations from 1983 to 1995; played in three World Cups winning a runners-up medal in 1987 and a bronze medal in 1995; played in six Five Nations championship-winning teams; shares the French Five Nations try-scoring record of 14 with Serge Blanco; is one of only five players to have scored a try in every match of a Five Nations championship; was inducted into the International Rugby Hall of Fame in 1999 and the International Rugby Board Hall of Fame in 2008.

Almost. What the statistics don't tell us is that Sella was one of those extraordinarily valuable players whose work rate, accuracy and effectiveness were as evident in defence as they were on attack, who was both rock and rapier, and who combined utter dependability with the X-factor, thus ensuring his place among the game's greatest-ever midfield backs.

Heroes inspire their team-mates to get off their knees when their bodies scream for relief and to be better players than they thought they were.

Nor do the statistics convey the absolute admiration and respect in which Sella was held by team-mates and opponents alike, not merely because of his greatness as a player but because he embodied the spirit of rugby.

He came from a sporting family: his uncle was a basketball player and his father a cyclist who also played on the wing for Clairac, the club where Sella began his career playing for the under-10 rugby league team.

"My dream was to play for Agen, which is 30 kilometres away," says Sella. "They were a good club who played a nice brand of rugby that I liked to watch – running rugby with flair. I joined as a 17-year-old and played for France under-18 against Scotland in Glasgow with Eric Champ. David Sole and Gavin Hastings were in the Scottish team. I was dropped after that game but, the following year, I played for France under-19 as a wing. I was quite quick when I was young."

Those who marked him throughout his glittering career would attest that he remained pretty quick, in addition to being skilful, beautifully balanced, clever, deceptively strong and physically and mentally hard.

Sella has remained involved with rugby, not only as manager of the France under-20 team, but also as an expert commentator on the Canal Plus network and as an ambassador and advertisement for the game: "Rugby is about meeting people, commitment, involvement, well-being, *joie de vivre*, effort. It is happiness, quite simply."

Virtually every rugby fan knows that Joel Stransky kicked the drop-goal in extra time that won the epic 1995 World Cup final and thereby earned the adulation of a nation and a place in the Springbok pantheon.

previous: Philippe Sella (France)   above: Sean Fitzpatrick (New Zealand)

"What you remember is getting there: the journey. Winning the World Cup is great but that's not what it's about. When we were wandering around the field after the final, it would have mattered half a per cent to me if we hadn't won because doing it is what it's all about."

MARTIN JOHNSON

But there are other things about Stransky that aren't so well known.

For instance, it may not be known that up till the very last minute he was by no means a certainty for the Springbok squad, having been originally left out of the team for a warm-up game against Manu Samoa.

That in the opening match of the tournament, against Australia, he became the first Springbok in history to score in all four possible ways – try, conversion, penalty, drop-goal – in the same test. Or that he scored all of South Africa's 15 points in the final. Or that prior to the tournament he'd never dropped a goal in an international match.

Or that, during his three-season stint with English club Leicester (1997–1999), he gave serious thought to making himself available for England on the basis of an English-born grandfather. As it turned out, it was his great-grandfather who was born in England.

Or that he is one of ten Jews to have played for the Springboks. After Aaron 'Okey' Geffin had kicked the Springboks to a series whitewash of the All Blacks in 1949, Springbok coach Dr Danie Craven, the Godfather of South African rugby, declared that it was good luck to have a Jew in the team. Craven's words have always carried great weight in South African rugby. After Stransky's drop-goal, they must have attained the status of pronouncements from on high.

Or that he once told off the screen giant Clint Eastwood for interrupting his speech. It happened at a dinner during the filming of Invictus, the Eastwood-directed film about the 1995 World Cup. Eastwood's late entrance caused considerable distraction among the audience, hence Stransky's admonishment. This gives him the distinction of either being very brave or one of the few people in the Western world who wouldn't recognise Clint Eastwood if he walked into the room.

These days, Stransky, a prominent businessman, remains involved in rugby as an expert commentator on the South African Supersport network. He looks back on his own career and the advent of professionalism with few regrets.

"I think I could have been a better player. At times I probably enjoyed life. I enjoyed travelling, trying new things, meeting new people. I think the modern player is much more focused than we were, perhaps because he's paid to be. Having the ability to live, eat, sleep and think rugby creates focus. But rugby took me to some fantastic places and I wouldn't change that for the world."

In November 2010, Stransky travelled to Washington DC to accept a Common Ground Award from the Search for Common Ground organisation on behalf of the 1995 Springboks. Their award recognises their role in inspiring unity and healing through the power of sport.

Interviewed after the ceremony, Stransky explained how a group of rugby players managed the difficult balancing act of winning a tournament and responding to the yearning for reconciliation and national unity that existed in South Africa after the dismantling of apartheid and the election of Nelson Mandela.

"We were just a bunch of young sportsmen wanting to get out on the field and do the best we could. But we had a common goal and a little slogan we tried to live by: one team, one country."

The rest, as they say, is history. And history is made by heroes.

'Pride' is the Dr Jekyll and Mr Hyde of the English language: there's good pride and there's bad pride.

In the Collins English Dictionary, the negative – "Excessive self-esteem; conceit" – is sandwiched between two positives: "A feeling of honour and self-respect; a sense of personal worth" and "Satisfaction or pleasure taken in one's own or another's success, achievements, etc."

PRIDE

"The whole point of rugby is that it is, first and foremost, a state of mind, a spirit."

JEAN-PIERRE RIVES

In general usage, the negative connotation is prominent, perhaps as a result of its association with the ultra-negative 'prejudice' in the title of one of the best-loved novels in the English language, Jane Austen's *Pride and Prejudice*. Or it may be the residual influence of Sunday School or religious education classes, where we were taught that "pride goeth before destruction, and an haughty spirit before a fall" (Proverbs, chapter 16, verse 18).

In rugby union, though, pride is almost exclusively a positive term. We talk about "pride in the jersey" and players are happy to describe themselves, or be described, as "a proud Wasp", "a proud Waratah", "a proud Springbok".

previous, top right: An Irish player surrounded by fans   previous, bottom right: After a Lions and Leopards match in South Africa   right: Tana Umaga and Jerry Collins (New Zealand)

John Mitchell, a well-travelled, high-profile coach, is an iconic figure in Waikato rugby in New Zealand, having played 134 games for the Mooloo men, 86 of them as captain. In 1993, aged 29, he was a surprise choice for the All Blacks tour of England and Scotland, on which he skippered the midweek team.

In his autobiography, All Black winger and full-back Jeff Wilson recalled the immense pride of this provincial stalwart whose hopes and expectations had never extended beyond taking part in an All Black trial. "Though I doubt Mitchell was ever close to making the test team, he was an immensely proud All Black. I remember him the night of the game in Gateshead when players, changed into casual clothes, were scattered all over Gateshead and across the Tyne in Newcastle, unwinding as only rugby players can. Mitchell sat quietly at the bar in our hotel, still dressed in his number ones. Asked why he hadn't changed and gone with his teammates, he replied simply and proudly, 'I don't know if I'll get another chance to wear this gear, so I'll just savour it while I can'."

And for those who insist that pride in representing one's country isn't what it used to be, herewith an excerpt from former Wallaby hooker Adam Freier's passionate defence of his generation in a 2010 column for the Australian website RugbyHeaven.com:

"We are constantly criticised and, from all reports, have no pride in our strip. Nonsense. When I had the honour of playing for the Wallabies, I would always get dressed last. I would look around the room and watch each of my team-mates slide their arms through the gold blanket of our code. There was a sense of pride. Digby Ioane would hang his number on his locker and simply sit and stare at it. Lote Tuqiri was the same and would often clutch it as if it was the first test he had played. It was the most beautiful thing to see grown men love something so much."

The jersey connects today's players to all those who went before, to the hundred-year legacy.

"When I had the honour of playing for the Wallabies, I would always get dressed last. I would look around the room and watch each of my team-mates slide their arms through the gold blanket of our code. There was a sense of pride."

ADAM FREIER

"I have kept every one of the Wallabies jerseys I played in. I would never take them to the dry-cleaners or put them into the team kitbag to get washed. Never would I give anything away for which I had worked so hard. It would never leave my sight. On tour I would wash it myself at the hotel in the shower, on the ever-slight chance it might get stolen or the colour would run."

"I can handle people questioning the form or the ability of a Wallaby, but to question their character and their pride in their country is another matter."

The jersey connects today's players to all those who went before, to the hundred-year legacy. Being an heir to that legacy is obviously a source of pride and inspiration, but it also carries a heavy responsibility.

Martin Johnson gained firsthand experience of the New Zealand rugby culture as a young man, representing King Country and playing for the 1990 New Zealand Colts team, which defeated the Australia under-21s, alongside the likes of Craig Dowd and Va'aiga Tuigamala.

"The All Blacks use their history – the idea that you can't let the jersey down, you can't be the team that fails to live up to the legacy," he says. "They've been able to use that tradition of success as a real positive."

Philippe Sella has no doubt that the single-mindedness with which the All Blacks approached the inaugural

World Cup in 1987, and their resolve when they faced France in the final, was a result of their defeat and physical humbling at the hands of the same opponents at Nantes the previous year. "That defeat helped the All Blacks to win the World Cup. Because they lost, they had a greater motivation; because we won, we didn't think about it in that sense."

Sometimes, however, the weight of history along with the public's and the media's tendency to mythologise the old heroes and hark back to the glory days can be a burden rather than an inspiration.

Martin Johnson believes: "For the Welsh teams who came after that golden era of the 1970s, the legacy was like a millstone around their necks: history weighed them down rather than inspired them. There's no doubt that the burden of expectation can be hard to handle."

For Australian Nick Farr-Jones, pride in the jersey and the legacy means being true to the way rugby has been imagined, interpreted and put into practice in one's country over the years, to a style of play that is distinctly your own. This, he argues, is not an airy-fairy or romantic notion – the opposite, in fact. Over time, a national style of play has emerged which suits the physical attributes and temperament of that nation's rugby players. Because it's based on doing what comes naturally, you depart from it at your peril.

"The privilege of pulling on the jersey and belting out the anthem."

NICK FARR-JONES

"The first thing you see when you get off the plane in Suva," he says, "is rows of pearly white teeth. The Fijians play with that happy-go-lucky spirit, with smiles on their faces. They hate structure, hate scrums – they want the wind in their hair. Japan is quite the opposite: a structured culture. They love scrums and lineouts, precision and combinations. The French have *joie de vivre*; they love the fine things in life and have flair."

"England is a conservative society, full of striped suits, and they like to play a suffocating game. The Afrikaners are a tough, hard, conservative people with plenty of tickets on themselves and they play an arrogant game. New Zealanders are people of the land – what you see is what you get. I played them 20 times and always took some souvenirs home. They play hard, direct, confrontational football."

"What's quintessential about my country? Over the years we've struggled for ball and have evolved a 'damn the torpedoes, full steam ahead' type of game. We'll chance our arm. I think you should try to stay true to yourself and your culture. When you wear the gold jersey, you want to run with the ball and score tries."

"The further away from our 1991 World Cup win I get, the more I realise it was something special but, at the time, I felt a sense of deflation. We didn't play very well at the tournament. We beat Samoa 9–3 and really got out of jail in the quarterfinal against Ireland. Our performance against the All Blacks in the semi was our best by a country mile. In the final against England we scored one try from a rolling maul. We won through our defence,

scoring one lousy try. Hopefully people can't remember that now. The English also went away from their game but in the opposite direction. If they'd stayed true to themselves, they probably would've knocked us over."

"Twenty minutes into the celebrations, coach Bob Dwyer said that, if we were honest, we'd acknowledge that we hadn't played that well. He called upon us to show the world that we could play and we were a much better team in 1992."

But players wear a number of jerseys and perform in many different settings in the course of their careers. Johnson talks about playing in front of a packed house on a pristine pitch at Twickenham on Saturday, and then having to front up for a midweek club match in ankle-deep mud on a freezing night in front of a handful of spectators. This is where personal pride and the refusal to let your standards drop really count. Those who have the ability to draw a good performance out of themselves in such circumstances are likely to go further in rugby – and indeed in life – than those who lack that inner drive and personal pride.

"No matter who the coach is, he won't be everybody's cup of tea so you have to learn to push your own buttons; you can't depend on someone else to do it for you," says Johnson. "It's difficult because you can't play as if your life depends on it every week, so the challenge is being able to put in a performance when there isn't the stimulation of a big occasion with a lot of buzz and anticipation and a lot riding on it. Often the hardest games to get up for are those you're expected to win comfortably."

Remarkably, for a player universally acknowledged as one of the all-time greats, Sella sometimes suffered from a lack of confidence. He overcame that by looking within. "I think the key to my success was that I always questioned myself with a view to getting better," he says. "I prepared for games thinking about the environment, my team-mates, myself; I focused on the opposition and the game. You need to have a lot of confidence in yourself and I didn't always have that, so perhaps I compensated with my preparation and concentration on my individual role and team role."

The paradox of John Kirwan is that the pride which drove him to perform on the rugby field also drove him to move on in several senses once his playing days were over.

"I had a lot of great moments in my career: winning the Ranfurly Shield was a very special game; winning the Gallaher Shield with Marist who hadn't won it for 52 years; winning the Italian Championship with Treviso who hadn't won it for 15 years. I was very fortunate in that respect. But I'm not a person who thinks about yesterday. My great fear – and this was probably a by-product of suffering depression – was that I'd stop growing. Because being an All Black is such a big part of your life, I think that some players stop developing when they finish playing."

"If I wanted to come home and be JK Inc rather than work, it would be very easy and pretty lucrative. But I made a conscious decision that I wanted to keep growing; that I didn't want to be identified as an ex-All Black for the rest of my life."

"When you're ten years old kicking a football around the garden, you dream of being the hero, scoring the winning try, getting the glory."

JOEL STRANSKY

GLORY

Whether we like it or not – and many don't – these days there is no glory in rugby that compares to the glory of winning the World Cup.

When the notion of a Rugby World Cup was first mooted, its opponents – mainly administrators in the Four Home Unions – warned that it could take on a life of its own and mutate, like Dr Frankenstein's monster, into something far bigger and therefore harder to control than was ever intended.

Their primary concern was that a World Cup would lead inexorably to professionalism, first by increasing the playing load beyond what was reasonable to expect of amateurs and, second, by generating revenue of which the players were bound to demand a share.

They also argued that a World Cup would come to dominate the rugby landscape to the detriment of traditional tournaments and rivalries. Some even predicted that rugby would find itself following the soccer model in which the focus is always on the next World Cup and international fixtures in the interim are seen first and foremost as opportunities for experimentation and development.

previous: Bob Skinstad and Joe van Niekerk (South Africa)   right: Daniel Carter (New Zealand)

"I just tried to be the best I could be and enjoy what I was doing."

MARTIN JOHNSON

Thankfully, it hasn't come to that. The Six Nations tournament has retained its prestige and appeal, and thus remains the centrepiece of the northern hemisphere season. The British and Irish Lions' tours of New Zealand in 2005 and South Africa in 2009 were resounding successes, leaving fans in the host countries yearning for the restoration of old-fashioned tours. The Tri-Nations tournament struggles against the tyranny of distance but continues to produce high-quality competition, and will be enhanced by Argentina's participation.

Perhaps there's a hint of an undue preoccupation with the World Cup in the 'peaking too early' taunt directed at the All Blacks whenever they put together a string of good results a year or two out from the tournament. The implication is that success between tournaments is neither here nor there unless it culminates in triumph at the World Cup. It's also a convenient way of discounting someone else's success while putting a gloss on one's own lacklustre results.

Few have a better perspective on rugby's order of priorities than Martin Johnson, who experienced World Cup disappointment and glory as a player then, not long into well-earned retirement, took on the job of preparing England for the 2011 World Cup.

"For the two years leading into the 1999 World Cup, the England coaching group was making a big thing about it," he says. "It was all about the World Cup. When it actually arrived, it became quite difficult to deal with. There's a long time between World Cups, and you can actually have a pretty decent career in the interim. I believe you just have to concentrate on being competitive right now. I hate this line about peaking between World Cups. What are you supposed to do – lose so you eliminate the risk of peaking too early?"

"From 2000 through to the 2003 World Cup, we didn't lose against southern hemisphere opposition. You can look back now and see it as a measured, methodical build-up to the World Cup but the point is, we enjoyed those victories. They were big test matches. To win in the south is a big achievement. I was aware of what was ahead but I certainly never went along with the aim of peaking in 2003; I just tried to be the best I could be and enjoy what I was doing."

However, Johnson also makes the valid point that the focus on the World Cup and its dominance of the rugby calendar are partly by-products of the huge increase in the volume of international rugby. These days, international teams play around 15 tests a year and the 50 Caps club, not so long ago an exclusive fraternity, now has trouble keeping track of its membership.

"There's far more rugby played nowadays," says Johnson, "so maybe there's a disposable element to some of it in the sense that it's not going to linger in the memory. When I was young, the All Blacks only came to the UK every few years; now they come every year. We know they don't lose too often over here but who remembers actual games and score-lines? But every British and Irish rugby fan can remember details of the Lions' tours of New Zealand in 1971 and South Africa in 1974."

The World Cup is now such a huge event that it's easy to forget that the inaugural tournament in Australia and New Zealand in 1987 went off without a great deal of fanfare. Neither the players nor the public were quite sure what to make of it. There were 4,000 empty seats at the Australia–France semifinal at Sydney's Concord Oval where capacity was barely 20,000. Nick Farr-Jones didn't even stop work. He was getting up at 5am and going into the office until a suspicious Wallaby coach Alan Jones rang his direct line and was greeted with: "Nick Farr-Jones speaking".

And in the more self-effacing amateur era, glorious moments were often private triumphs celebrated in private. John Kirwan had a World Cup winner's medal on the mantelpiece but sought glory in self-improvement.

"I always thought of it in terms of working at something and finally getting it right," he says. "I was good at standing guys up and beating them on the inside or outside, but I didn't run angles that well. On the 1992 tour of Australia and South Africa, I was having a difficult time because I felt the coach didn't like me and wanted to get rid of me. I endlessly practised running angles and, in the last game against South Africa in Johannesburg, I scored a try by running a good angle. It was the fruition of months of practice. That for me was a glorious moment."

previous: Bryan Habana (South Africa) right: Martin Johnson (England)

above: Drew Mitchell (Australia)

above: Adam Ashley-Cooper (Australia)

above, top: Adam Ashley-Cooper (Australia) scores a try   above, bottom: Phil Waugh (Australia)   57

"Sport is a universal language, and triumph is always triumph, and disaster is always disaster."

SIMON BARNES

By kicking the drop-goal in extra time that secured the 1995 World Cup, Springbok Joel Stransky achieved a level of glory even beyond that of his team-mates. Perhaps that's why he's slightly uncomfortable with the concept.

"Glory is something the public and media talk about," he says, "but I don't think it's a word modern players use; it's something that comes after. When you're ten years old kicking a football around the garden, you dream of being the hero, scoring the winning try, getting the glory. But when you're actually out there participating at that level, you just concentrate on doing your job, doing the little things well. And when you do achieve a goal, you set new goals and move on."

South Africa's triumph at the 1995 World Cup was one of the most uplifting and glorious sporting achievements of modern times. Its historical significance was not lost on the wider world, hence the fact that it became the subject of the major motion picture *Invictus* directed by cinematic giant Clint Eastwood.

But personal glory and momentous social and political implications were far from the players' minds when they embarked on their World Cup campaign. Their guiding principle was that hoariest of sporting clichés: one game at a time.

"We set our goals six months in advance and worked our butts off," says Stransky. "Our first goal was to beat Australia in the opening game; by doing that we secured the easier route to the final. Winning the tournament then became a realistic goal and we reset our sights accordingly."

"At the time, it didn't feel as if we'd done this great unifying thing. We celebrated that night and woke up to find that the win had carried over into this overwhelming national celebration. We had the support of the country during a period of dramatic change centred on the election of a leader who not long before under apartheid had been perceived as a terrorist. We needed the World Cup victory to unite our country. Nelson Mandela used it for that purpose and the whole country came together around a sports team. Weeks afterwards, I realised that it wasn't just a sporting achievement; it had a national implication which led to the glory and celebrity."

But honeymoons are short-lived. The World Cup feel-good factor came up against hard political, social and economic reality. South African rugby made a series of missteps, frittering away much of the goodwill it had accrued. And like World Cup winners before and since, the heroes themselves discovered that when the golden glow faded, what remained was a curious feeling of emptiness.

right: Mils Muliaina (New Zealand) dives over the try-line

above: Richard Dourthe (France)

above, top: David Kirk (New Zealand)   above, bottom: Jason Robinson (England)   61

above: The All Blacks

above: Johnny O'Connor (Ireland)   63

There is no glory in rugby that compares to the glory of winning the World Cup.

"Motivational speakers and life trainers talk about personal growth and journeys," says Stransky. "When you set a goal like winning the World Cup, that becomes a journey. It lasts for a given length of time during which you're focused on a particular mission which gives you a reason to train hard. When it's over, there's this period when you think: what now? What's my focus tomorrow?"

"In 2010, I did an eight-day mountain-bike ride for charity. It's one of the hardest mountain-bike rides in the world, absolutely torturous. Finally it was over and I was having dinner with my family; instead of feeling 'Thank God that's over and done with', I found myself thinking, 'What am I going to do tomorrow?' You give something your absolute focus for a given period, then you wake up one morning and it's been taken away from you."

Such is the flipside of glory. The cup is in the trophy cabinet and the winner's medal can never be taken away, but the exhilarating sense of mission and comradeship has dissipated and must be rekindled for the next campaign.

And while the World Cup is unquestionably rugby union's Holy Grail, the game is a broad church in which amateurs and professionals, players from the traditional powerhouses and those from countries where rugby is a minority sport or a novelty, pursue their various goals and dare to dream. Not everyone can be a World Cup winner, but every rugby player has a quest which he or she hopes will have a happy and glorious ending.

As coach of Japan, John Kirwan pursues different goals to those he chased as an All Black but, should he and his team succeed, the glory will be comparable: "Our goal is to be a special team which means being in the top ten in the world and winning two games at the 2011 World Cup which no Japanese team has ever done. To do that would be a glorious achievement. We'll have a reunion in 20 years' time like the 1987 All Blacks did."

The passing of time has given Joel Stransky an admirable perspective, both on his own achievement and on the place of sporting glory in the grand scheme of things: "If I look back, I'd have to say I'd rather have kicked that drop-goal than not kicked it. I wasn't actually a great drop-kicker so, when I was young and egotistical, it irked me a little to be known just for that kick. Now it's just nice to be recognised."

"I'm always amazed and amused when the term 'legend' is applied to rugby players, and it seems to be applied more liberally with each passing year. To me, that status belongs to people like Nelson Mandela, Archbishop Desmond Tutu, Winston Churchill and the great explorers: the likes of Captain Cook. I'm not sure that sportsmen are worthy of that accolade."

A prominent South African coach once observed that, contrary to popular opinion, rugby union is not a contact sport.

"Ballroom dancing is a contact sport," he explained. "Rugby is a collision sport."

Rugby is often about skill, athleticism and acumen. Occasionally it's even about artistry. But it's always about the application of physical force.

Sometimes force is applied in an organised, controlled manner, for instance, when the forward packs crunch into each other at the set scrum hell-bent on gaining a physical and psychological edge. Referees call this 'the engage'; everyone else calls it 'the hit'.

COURAGE

"Ballroom dancing is a contact sport. Rugby is a collision sport."

Sometimes the collisions are as unpredictable as is a dodgem-car pile-up. Boxers fear the punch they don't see coming. The rugby field is a much more crowded and volatile environment than is the boxing ring; when you have the ball, you could be hit by any one – or more than one – of 15 opponents coming at you from all angles, including from your blind side.

You have to be courageous to play this game and courage comes from within. Like speed, courage is very difficult to coach.

"The only trophy we won this day, was the blood and sweat we left on the pitch... and it was enough."

Some rugby fans, not all of them senior citizens, complain that the game has gone soft. They yearn for a return to the good old days when men were men and referees just got out of the way and let them prove it. Leaving aside the fact that this red-misted nostalgia seems to blind the complainants to the shuddering physicality of the contemporary game, it sometimes veers uncomfortably close to eulogising thuggery.

Rugby journalists with space to fill during lulls in the season periodically compile lists of the great hard men, essentially a pretext for revisiting famous confrontations and notorious incidents. These exercises generally leave the impression that the journalists concerned have either forgotten or are too young to remember just how much bitterness these incidents generated at the time.

When rugby players reminisce, they tend to reserve their warmest admiration for those who sacrificed for the cause – put their bodies on the line, in the modern parlance – rather than those who were more interested in dishing it out.

That's why Ron Elvidge occupies a special place in the All Black pantheon. He captained New Zealand against the 1950 British Lions but, in the third test at Athletic Park, Wellington, was forced from the field with collarbone and facial injuries.

right: Richard Cockerill and Martin Johnson (Leicester)

above: Colin Meads (New Zealand) and Benoît Dauga (France)

If Rives were playing today, he'd spend half his career in the blood-bin.

There were no replacements in those days so the All Blacks were down to 14 men which became 13 when prop Johnny Simpson suffered a knee injury. With both the game and the series in the balance, Elvidge returned to the field. Although one arm was next to useless, he operated as an extra fullback and chimed into a backline move to score the try that won the game and sealed the series.

Elvidge never played rugby again. With injury ruling him out of the fourth and final test, he retired from the game to pursue a medical career which saw him become one of New Zealand's foremost gynaecologists.

Courage, like other less-admirable attributes, is universal. Mike Davis, an English second-row forward of the 1960s (and later an England coach) played on against the All Blacks despite a serious shoulder injury, prompting Colin Meads to describe him as "one of the most courageous locks I have played against".

And who can forget the inspirational Jean-Pierre Rives, the great French flanker and captain? He always stood out on the field, either because of his distinctive long, blond locks or because his head was swathed in bloodied bandages. If Rives were playing today, he'd spend half his career in the blood-bin.

John Kirwan has vivid memories of two extraordinary instances of self-sacrificial courage. Both came from All Black number eight Wayne 'Buck' Shelford, the talismanic captain who almost single-handedly transformed the haka from a diffident shuffle into a full-throated assertion of cultural identity and national pride.

In the third test against the Wallabies at Sydney's Concord Oval in 1988, Shelford suffered a horrendous head cut. "I was standing right next to him," says Kirwan. "It was the worst head wound I ever saw – blood spurting everywhere. Our team doctor, John 'Doc' Mayhew, came out onto the field, took one look and told Buck he'd have to go off. Buck said, 'Just put some Vaseline on it.'"

A dialogue of the deaf ensued with Shelford telling Mayhew to put some Vaseline on the cut while the doctor tried to get it through to him that he'd have to go off and get proper treatment, which would include multiple stitches.

Kirwan recalls: "Finally Buck said, 'If you don't give me some bloody Vaseline, they'll be carrying you off the field.' So Doc reluctantly handed over the jar; Buck took a big scoop, slapped it on the wound, and went back into the fray."

Which meant immediately putting his lacerated head into a scrum. It was an All Black feed: Shelford picked up the ball at the base of the scrum, put his head down, and charged. "He went 30 metres with about five of them hanging off him," says Kirwan. "After that I simply couldn't not be courageous – in fact, I would've done anything to win that game. When you witness raw courage like that, it has a galvanising effect on you."

The All Blacks–France test at La Beaujoire Stadium in Nantes in 1986 was one of the most brutal matches of all time. So ferocious was the French onslaught that Shelford later speculated, perhaps in jest, about what was in their water bottles. Given what happened, it's not surprising that he was still wondering what hit him.

With a few minutes to go, Shelford left the field, which was unusual, if not unheard of. After the game, no one in the shell-shocked dressing-room had the nerve to ask the question that was on everyone's mind: what exactly had forced this apparently indestructible warrior off the field?

Kirwan says: "Eventually I just blurted it out: 'Buck, what happened to you, mate?' He said he'd had a couple of teeth knocked out then added, as a sort of afterthought, 'Oh yeah, and this'. He pulled down his shorts: his scrotum was split in two." In the deathly hush that followed, Shelford explained that the injury had happened in the second minute "but it got to the stage where I just couldn't stand it any more".

Kirwan's abiding memory of that night is getting back to the hotel after the formal dinner to find Shelford, who'd been at the local hospital getting 40-odd stitches in his scrotum, standing at the bar "with his legs a long way apart".

"People mightn't think so, but when you're out there in the cauldron with enormous pressure on you, including the self-imposed pressure not to let your mates and your country down, it requires courage to put fear aside and take a risk, do something bold."

JOHN KIRWAN

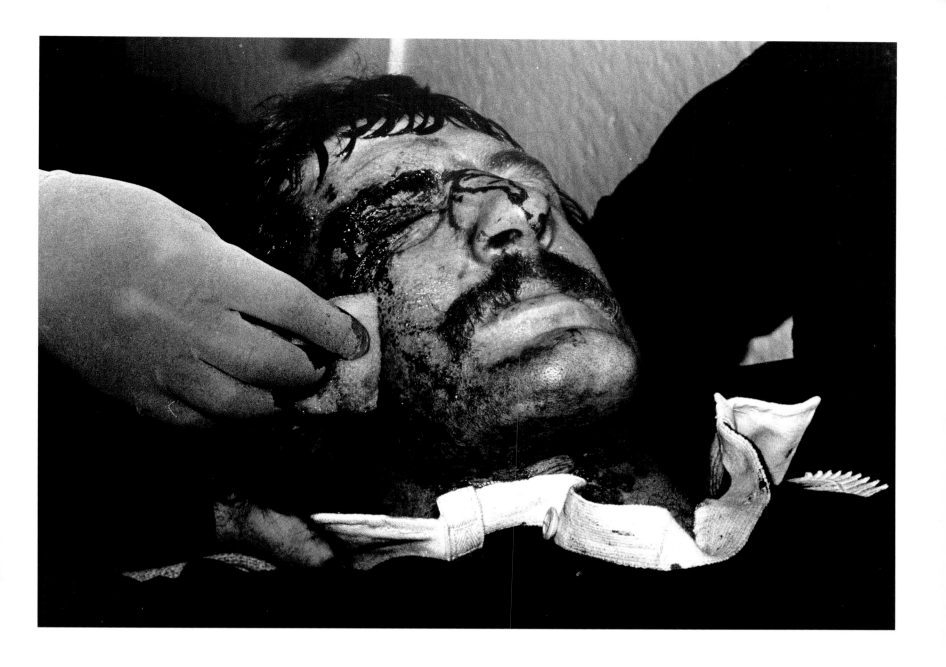

"Without violence there is no courage, without mayhem there is no grace, without pain there is no exalted relief in victory."

SIMON BARNES

above: Yannick Jauzion (France) tackles Luke McAlister (New Zealand)   right: Keith Wood (Ireland) is stopped by Jason Leonard and Richard Hill (England)

next, left: Jonny Wilkinson (England) and John Smit (South Africa)   next, right: George Gregan (Australia) and Keith Wood (Ireland)   79

You have to be courageous to play this game and courage comes from within.

But Kirwan is quick to point out that courage comes in two forms. There is physical courage, which is highly visible and often spectacular and therefore gets most of the attention; and then there is mental courage, which is harder to recognise and quantify.

"People mightn't think so," he says, "but when you're out there in the cauldron with enormous pressure on you, including the self-imposed pressure not to let your mates and your country down, it requires courage to put fear aside and take a risk, do something bold. It takes courage to express yourself under pressure, especially if your confidence is down. In some ways, going through the pain barrier is easier."

Joel Stransky agrees: "You expect players at the top to be courageous in the physical contact aspects of the game – scrum, breakdown, tackle, getting over the gain line and so on. There's a further step into what you might call mental courage – the captain who kicks for the corner to set up a lineout rather than taking a shot at goal; the kicker who goes for the corner rather than playing safe and just making sure he puts it out in the field of play; the guy who's willing to throw the ten-metre pass across the face of an advancing defence; the hooker who throws to the back of the lineout knowing that Victor Matfield's going to contest."

right: Lawrence Dallaglio (England) and Tana Umaga (New Zealand)

above: Justin Bishop (Ireland) is tackled by Tim Horan (Australia)

above: Mud and guts (match and location unknown)

"Playing rugby at school, I once fell on a loose ball and, through ignorance and fear, held on despite a fierce pummelling. After that it took me months to convince my team-mates I was a coward."

PETER COOK

right: John Philip 'Bakkies' Botha (South Africa) at the bottom of a maul

above: George Smith (Australia) at the bottom of a ruck

above: *Os du Randt (South Africa) barges George Gregan (Australia)* 93

"The key is to ensure that the fear of failure doesn't overshadow the courage to go out and win. You must have the courage to go out to win rather than not to lose."

JOEL STRANSKY

"There are so many little decisions. Once they've been made, you have to execute, which is where the physical courage comes in. The modern player is challenged in so many ways: the game is quicker, he has less time and space in which to make decisions and execute, and the consequences of getting it wrong are dire."

Which brings us to the Rugby World Cup where the stakes are higher, the pressure greater and the consequences of errors in decision-making and execution don't bear thinking about. Given all that, is sticking to your attacking guns courageous or simply foolish?

While admitting that northern hemisphere conditions tend to encourage a more limited style of play, England's Martin Johnson argues that history offers a very clear lesson: World Cups are won by pragmatism rather than by razzle-dazzle.

"The pressure of knockout games at the World Cup tends to dictate a style of play aimed at minimising

mistakes and depriving the opposition of opportunities. Caution takes over. Games like the 1999 France–New Zealand semifinal are the exception, not the rule. If you blow someone away, well and good, but it doesn't happen often; winning by a few points is the rule. Two finals have been won by drop-goals in extra time; in 1999, Australia kicked a drop-goal in extra time to make the final."

"Look at soccer: to win the World Cup you're likely to have to win at least one game along the way by penalty shootout. That's just the nature of these tournaments which have assumed huge importance. It's rarely going to be about playing expansively but, rather, executing the fundamentals well under pressure. Isolate the game and play it. In my country we have this constant debate about winning with style but, in my book, good rugby is winning rugby."

Stransky steers a middle course, acknowledging the case for pragmatism but arguing that conservatism

has its own risks. "When the stakes are high," he says, "there's always the temptation to play safe, play the percentages, avoid risks – that way you don't expose yourself to the risk of making the mistake that costs your team, your country, the World Cup. The key is to ensure that the fear of failure doesn't overshadow the courage to go out and win. You must have the courage to go out to win rather than not to lose."

But Kirwan, the romantic, insists that New Zealand must have the courage to be true to its legacy and to itself: "It will take courage for the All Blacks to go to a World Cup when they haven't won it for over 20 years and play an expansive style of rugby. They could win it by kicking the leather off the ball and bashing people, but that's not being true to our roots and the way we want to play the game."

right: Schalk Burger (South Africa) and Akapusi Qera and Vilimoni Delasau (Fiji)   next: Shane Geraghty (England) and Christophe Dominici (France)

"The greatest feeling I have ever had as a coach is walking into the changing rooms and seeing the grins on their faces and the enjoyment."

WAYNE SMITH

TEAM

More than any other sport, rugby union is a game for all shapes and sizes.

There are two very different set pieces – the scrum and lineout – each of which requires specific skill sets and physical attributes. There is a clear demarcation between backs and forwards, with both units consisting of three distinct 'departments'. The backline is made up of a back three, a midfield and halves; up front there's a back row (loose forwards), a second row (locks) and a front row.

Though the modern game requires multi-skilled players who are adept and comfortable away from their specialist roles – tight forwards who can catch and pass, and backs who can clean out at the breakdown – and even though there will always be players whose physiques

don't fit the mould, the core duties of each department suit identifiable body shapes and physical attributes.

By contrast, rugby league, lacking a meaningful set piece or indeed any contest for possession, seems to be evolving into a game for homogenous teams of inter-changeable players in which the number on the jersey is almost irrelevant.

"Rugby is a very inclusive game," says Nick Farr-Jones. "There's a position for every physical type: tall guys, squat guys, little scuttlers, giraffes and greyhounds. You need minders, binders and grinders – it's all about working out what your strengths are and doing your job, surrounding yourself with people who become your team."

As they say in France, a rugby team needs piano players and piano movers.

Perhaps no nation better illustrates a rugby team's capacity for accommodating physical difference than France. The mythology surrounding French rugby is largely concerned with flair and *joie de vivre* – the great tradition of sleight of hand and thrilling attack initiated by diminutive and nimble inside backs like Jean Gachassin and Pierre *'Monsieur Le Drop'* Albaladejo, advanced by dashing midfielders like the Boniface brothers, André and Guy, Jo Maso and Philippe Sella, and finished by gliding athletes like Pierre Villepreux and Serge Blanco.

But there's another side to the coin. Only the Argentineans revere the scrum as much as the French do, and this devotion to the dark arts is reflected in generations of men whose barrel-chested pugnacity belongs to an entirely different tradition: one as macho as any in the game.

All Black second-rower Colin Meads, as uncompromising a forward as ever stampeded into a ruck, rated his French opponents physically harder than the South Africans. "The French leave their mark on you," he said. In his case, it was a huge gash on the side of his head courtesy of the notorious Alain Plantefol at Stade Colombes, Paris, in 1967.

The French pack of the mid-to-late-1970s was one of the most technically proficient, physically imposing, hard-nosed units ever to take to the field. After being chewed up and spat out in Paris in 1976, the Wallaby forwards expressed utter shock at the intensity of the pressure brought to bear on them in the scrums.

There was the 'Beast of Béziers', the towering, biblically bearded lock, Alain Esteve. His second-row partner Michel Palmié was banned for life for partially blinding an opponent in a club game. He went on to become a prominent administrator. Loosehead prop Gérard Cholley, an ex-paratrooper, was a late starter. According to legend, he was spotted by a rugby coach while plying his trade as a fairground boxer. After Cholley had felled three members of the Scottish pack on the same afternoon, a reporter described him as "moving up and down the lineout like a bus conductor punching tickets".

Cholley's predecessor in the Tricolours' front row was Armand Vaquerin, who later tragically died playing Russian roulette in his own bar in Béziers (*Le Cardiff*). An annual pre-season tournament is named after him.

But for all the contradictory mystique of French rugby and it's penchant for doing things in it's own, inimitably Gallic way, Philippe Sella's approach to the game and sense of team would resonate with players the world over. As rugby people know, there's no 'I' in team. "I looked to play my best for the team," he says. "It wasn't important to me whether I touched the ball or not, because in that case I could make a contribution defensively. You need to be good for the team whatever the circumstances and the nature of the game."

"When I was young watching and listening to the French team sing *La Marseillaise* before the game was a powerful feeling. When you are in that position, you think of the players who've gone before you who may be watching you now, and that produces a strong emotion. But when I started with the French team, we didn't sing the anthem for several years. Maybe we were shy but we didn't sing even though we had the cockerel in our hearts. Then at the beginning of the 1990s, we began to sing, which was much better because you're stronger together as a team and more involved with the supporters."

Rugby discussion and literature abounds with references to the Latin temperament. It certainly used to be the case that the French team's discipline wasn't all it should have been. One of Sella's unhappiest memories is the 18–17 loss to Scotland at Murrayfield, Edinburgh, in the 1986 Five Nations, which cost France a Grand Slam.

"We scored tries," he says, "Scotland didn't. But they won because our discipline let us down. Our discipline wasn't always the best, perhaps because what was okay in our domestic rugby wasn't okay in international rugby, and we often failed to make the adjustment."

It could be argued that given the lax refereeing and wild indiscipline that used to be the norm in French domestic rugby, their discipline in international matches was, on the whole, creditable.

"There's a position for every physical type: tall guys, squat guys, little scuttlers, giraffes and greyhounds."

NICK FARR-JONES

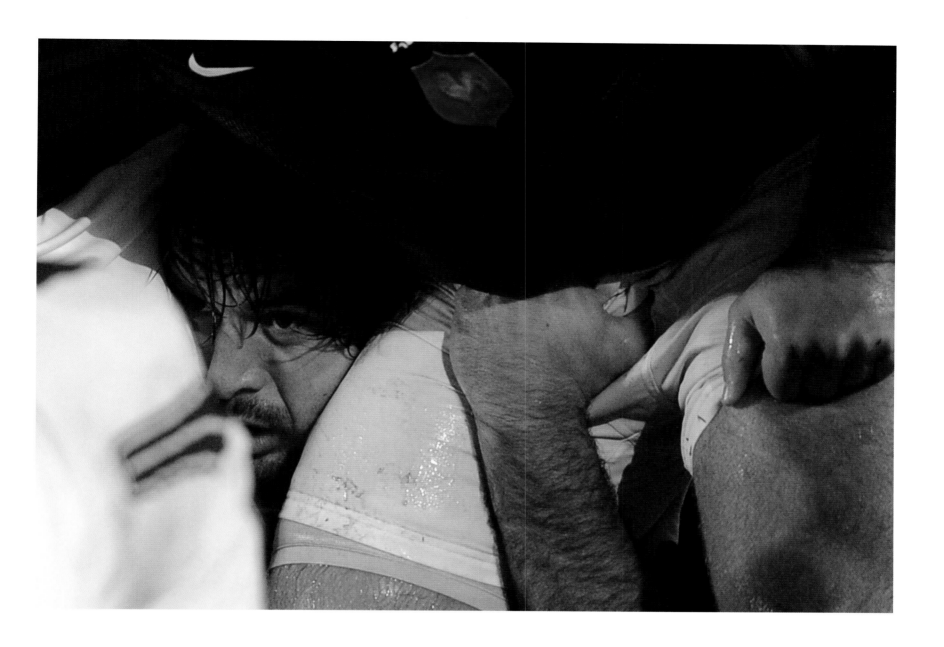

"It wasn't important to me whether I touched the ball or not, because in that case I could make a contribution defensively. You need to be good for the team whatever the circumstances and the nature of the game."

PHILIPPE SELLA

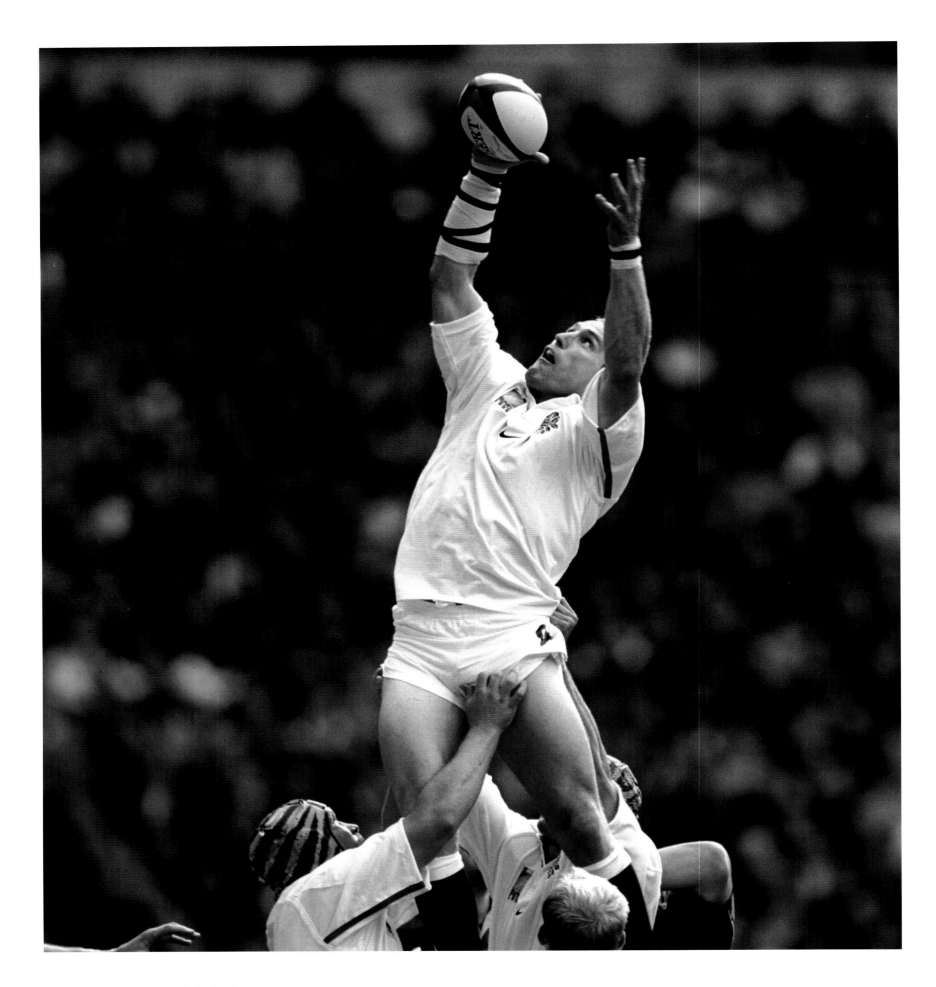

above: Lawrence Dallaglio (England)

above: Ireland and Wales players   next: Julien Bonnaire (France) falls as Ryan Jones (Wales) grabs the ball   109

"Remember that rugby is a team game; all 14 of you make sure you pass the ball to Jonah."

NEW ZEALAND SUPPORTER'S FAX TO THE ALL BLACKS AT THE 1995 WORLD CUP

The language barrier cannot be underestimated, however. The laws of rugby are complex and open to interpretation. How often do we see penalised players wandering away from breakdowns or collapsed scrums shaking their heads in mystification? Sometimes it's theatrics and sometimes they're simply in denial, but all too often the bewilderment is genuine. And how often have we seen games simmer and eventually come to the boil because one side – or perhaps both – has become frustrated by what they regard as nitpicking, incompetence or even bias on the referee's part?

Imagine the bewilderment and frustration if the referees were making and explaining their decisions in a foreign language?

There's a story, perhaps apocryphal but illustrative nonetheless, of an English club team playing a pre-season game in France. The referee was a local whose command of English was as shaky as was their command of French. The visitors quickly got offside with him, literally and metaphorically; try as they might to get back onside, the penalties kept coming. The visiting captain made little attempt to conceal his low opinion of the referee, who eventually took umbrage and ordered him from the field. The Englishman looked the referee in the eye and told him: "You can get stuffed!" With a regretful shake of his head, the Frenchman replied: "Zees apology comes too late".

Farr-Jones' greatest regret in rugby was losing to the British Lions in 1989. "Lions' tours come around once every 12 years, so you get one roll of the dice."

In hindsight, he sees that heartbreaking loss as an important step in the Wallabies' evolution from a brilliant but erratic outfit into a physically and mentally hardened team of World Cup winners.

"Inconsistency was one of the issues the Wallaby team of the late-1980s had to deal with as individuals and as a team. We had to ensure that passion and arousal and desperation to win didn't translate into scoreboard anxiety – trying things just to get the scoreboard moving. The team had to change its culture and become process-driven: do the job to the best of your ability, minimise errors and then, as difficult as it is, look up at the score-board at the end of 80 minutes and see what it tells you."

For John Kirwan, the essence of team is similar to the Australasian ethos of mateship. "I often say rugby's like life," he says. "You can have the ball in your hand and be running down the field feeling unstoppable. Then someone tackles you and you hit the deck and you're vulnerable; you're lying there exposed. Suddenly your team-mates are there, not just over the ball but over you, protecting you. They're prepared to put their bodies on the line for you. That's what happens in life: you fall over and your mates come to your aid."

Professionalism often gets a bad rap, accused of eroding traditional values and creating a breed of ruthlessly self-interested players with no permanent loyalties. Drawing on his long experience with the Leicester Tigers both as an amateur and a professional, Martin Johnson explains that the transition actually created tighter teams and closer personal bonds. "Before club rugby went professional, everybody had jobs and families, and players didn't necessarily live in the area because they lived closer to their jobs and we only trained twice a week. That meant you didn't necessarily see your team-mates that much. With professionalism, rugby was the job so players tended to live in the area. Plus, you were bringing in players from other parts of the country or overseas who didn't have friends and a network, so their social circle tended to be the other players. That era was really enjoyable because we became like a family – we socialised after training, after games and during the week. Those guys I played and socialised with for ten years became very good friends and still are."

"I often say rugby's like life. You can have the ball in your hand and be running down the field feeling unstoppable. Then someone tackles you and you hit the deck and you're vulnerable; you're lying there exposed. Suddenly your team-mates are there, not just over the ball but over you, protecting you. They're prepared to put their bodies on the line for you. That's what happens in life: you fall over and your mates come to your aid."

JOHN KIRWAN

right: Josh Lewsey and Lawrence Dallaglio (England)

"We became like a family... Those guys I played and socialised with for ten years became very good friends and still are."

MARTIN JOHNSON

above: The French team celebrates

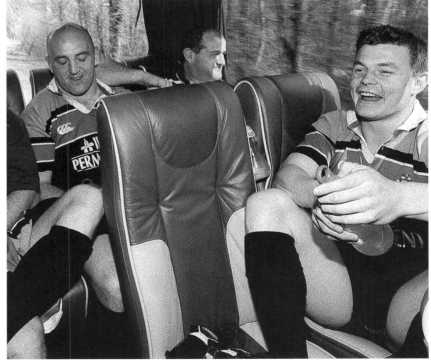

above, top: Chris de Nysschen (South Africa) above, bottom left: Players at Esher baths, England above, bottom right: Keith Wood, Peter Clohessy and Brian O'Driscoll (Ireland) 117

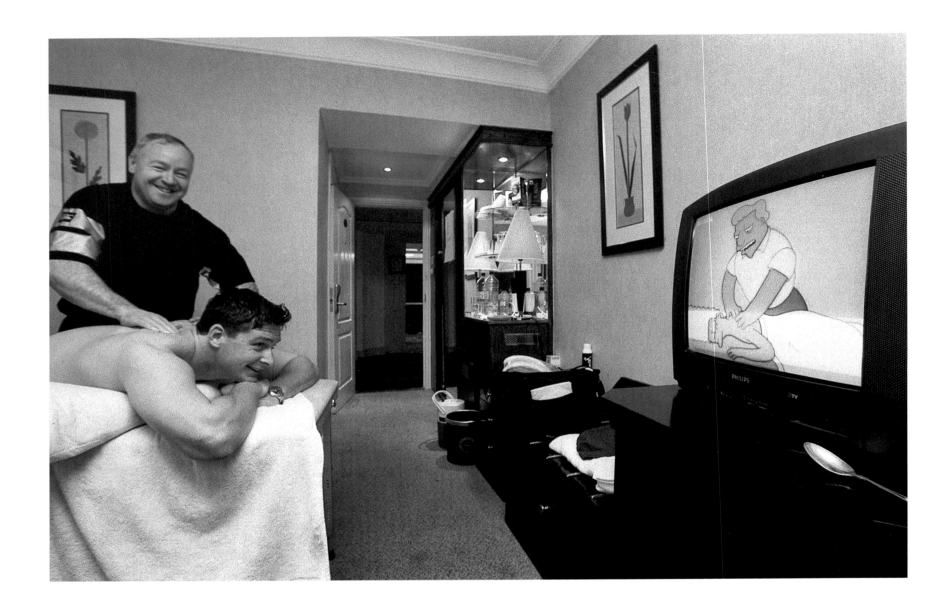

The public probably has a rose-tinted view of sports teams that achieve great things, seeing them as bands of brothers who remain close friends for life, assuming that their love of the game and shared triumphs override the factors that usually shape relationships. The reality is more complicated.

"I'm not terribly sure what team spirit is," says David Kirk, who captained the 1987 World Cup-winning All Blacks. "I know that teams that aren't winning aren't very happy."

Conversely, winning teams rise above personality clashes and prickly personal relationships. Asked about the prospects of the great Auckland team of the 1980s having a 20-year reunion, Kirk responded: "I wouldn't have a beer with some of them next Thursday night, let alone

in 20 years' time. Having said that, I think we had a good team spirit."

But the fans' romantic view is not entirely without substance. Though team bonds don't necessarily supersede the usual building blocks of friendship – compatibility, common interests, a shared sense of humour – they nonetheless exercise a lasting hold.

"I'm in touch with some of my team-mates from the 1995 World Cup-winning team," says Joel Stransky. "When you see each other, it's like you've never missed a day. It's a strong, tight relationship but, as men do, you don't always make the effort. There are some guys I played with that I never want to see again, but I have a couple of very good mates from my playing days. The friends I gained from rugby are friends for life."

Kirwan has a similar perspective: "People say to me that I must be great mates with the 1987 World Cup team. I'm not really. The only one I see on a regular basis is Joe Stanley. But if they walked in here tomorrow, it would be like there'd been no gap. Some of them aren't my type of people, but there's an enduring bond and a lifelong friendship based on respect."

"When tighthead prop John Drake passed away, we all vowed to stay in touch. In reality you don't, but it brought the whole question of friendship into focus. You're not necessarily friends with these guys in a conventional sense, but there's this bond that's hard to describe. Rugby friendships are hard to recapture in other parts of life because they're friendships forged in high-pressure situations when you're working towards a common goal."

above: Juan Martin Fernandez Lobbe and Juan Manuel Leguizamon (Argentina)

above, top: Juan Manuel Leguizamon (Argentina)   above, bottom: Serge Betsen hugs Dimitri Yachvili (France)   123

"In my time, I've had my knee out, broken my collar-bone, had my nose smashed, a rib broken, lost a few teeth, and ricked my back; but as soon as I get a bit of bad luck I'm going to quit the game."

J ROBINSON

PAIN

The late, lamented Warren Zevon, of *Werewolves of London* fame, wasn't your usual pop star.

He wrote songs about the perils of the one-night stand (*Poor, Poor Pitiful Me*) and the dead-end existence of the barfly (*Desperadoes Under the Eaves*), about soldiers of fortune (*Roland the Headless Thompson Gunner*) and teenage psychopaths (*Excitable Boy*), and about the sun setting on the British Empire (*Leave My Monkey Alone*) and shining on the American Empire (*The Envoy*).

He even wrote songs about sport: *Hit Somebody!* is about an ice hockey enforcer, and *Boom Boom Mancini* traces the career of the former world lightweight boxing champion and American folk hero Ray Mancini.

Boom Boom Mancini contains a line that will resonate with rugby players and followers the world over: "Some have the speed and the right combinations, but if you can't take the punches, it don't mean a thing."

right: Mof Myburgh (Northern Transvaal)

To succeed in rugby, as in boxing, you have to be able to take the pain. You have to be able to absorb punishment and keep coming.

Bobby Windsor, the man in the middle of the famous Pontypool front row, recently topped the *Western Mail*'s list of the hardest men in Welsh rugby history. He told the newspaper that, if he deserved the accolade, it was because of his ability to take punishment rather than dish it out.

His most painful encounters were at the hands – and feet and teeth – of the French pack of the mid-1970s, one of the roughest, toughest, meanest outfits ever assembled. They saw the hooker as the arrowhead of the opposition scrum: blunt the arrowhead, blunt the scrum.

When scrummaging against them, Windsor often didn't bind on his tighthead prop so that he could use his right arm to ward off the punches. When one of the French front-rowers kept trying to bite his ear, Windsor told his loosehead to deal with the carnivore. Unfortunately, the payback punch landed just as the Frenchman was taking another bite, and the resultant wrench caused a laceration requiring 16 stitches.

A French newspaper reported the incident under the headline: "*Windsor à la carte*".

Although few were better at dishing it out than was Colin Meads, his unofficial status as the greatest All Black of all time owes more to the indomitable spirit that drove him to play with a half-healed broken arm in South Africa in 1970 and return to the playing field at the age of 36 a few months after breaking several vertebrae and having the skin scraped off his back in a serious road accident. Perhaps, though, a curious off-field incident during the 1971 British Lions' tour of New Zealand best illustrates what Irish halfback-turned-journalist Andrew Mulligan meant when he wrote that Meads "knew no limit to the drive of the mind over his own matter".

In the match against the combined King Country–Wanganui team, Welsh number eight Mervyn Davies speared his bony shoulder into Meads' ribs as he stretched up for the ball. Blindsided, Meads wasn't prepared for what was a severe impact. He got back to his feet, giving Davies a stare that caused his bowels to flutter. For the rest of the game, the Welshman avoided the dark places where retribution surely awaited.

When Meads, still wearing an expression of narrow-eyed menace, approached Davies at the after-match function, the Lion feared he'd underestimated the man's implacability. With no apparent effort, Meads picked Davies up, bounced him in his arms like an infant, and set him down on his feet, acknowledging that he'd been well and truly nailed that afternoon.

It turned out that Meads had sustained a sprung rib cartilage as a result of Davies' shoulder charge. When news of the injury broke, Lions manager Dr Doug Smith, a medical man, told Davies that Meads' apparently playful gesture would have caused him intense pain.

To succeed in rugby, as in boxing, you have to be able to take the pain. You have to be able to absorb punishment and keep coming.

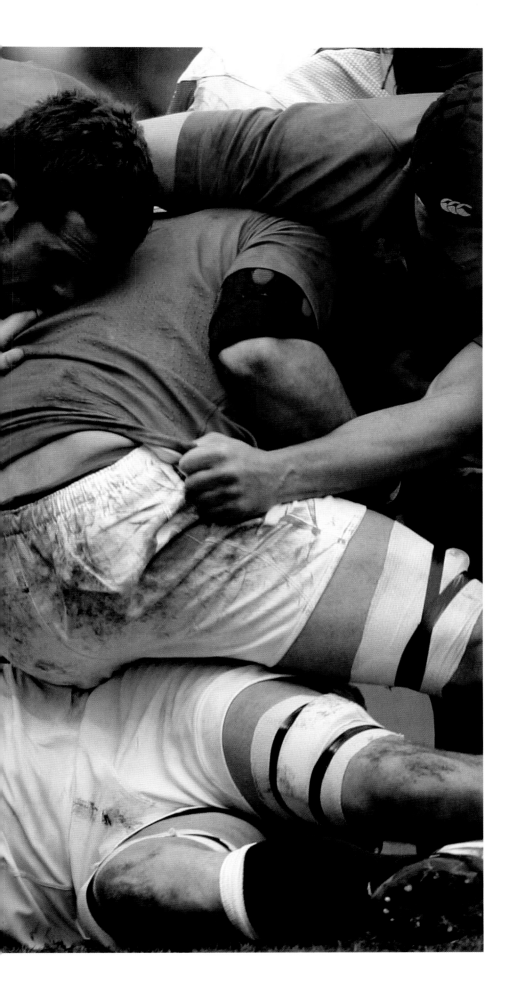

"Rugby is a game for big buggers. If you're not a big bugger, you get hurt. I wasn't a big bugger but I was a fast bugger and therefore I avoided the big buggers."

SPIKE MILLIGAN

Philippe Sella remembers the basic details of his international debut – it was against Romania in Bucharest on 31 October 1982 – but little else. Early on he dived on a loose ball just as a Romanian player went to hack it down the field. He woke up at 10pm that night.

Something similar happened five years later when France played Zimbabwe at Eden Park in Auckland in the inaugural World Cup. Within five minutes of coming off the substitutes' bench, Sella was kicked in the head and woke up in the dressing-room: "Someone told me we were at the World Cup and had been in New Zealand for three weeks. I didn't believe him."

At that tournament, Sella also suffered the emotional pain of losing the final a week after the euphoria of defeating Australia in an epic semifinal in Sydney.

"Before the game we gathered behind the goalposts and spoke about our friends, families and supporters back home. The passion was very strong but I believe some players were over-emotional and the final was partly lost there before the game had even started. Emotion is fine if it gets you happy and motivated, but too much is difficult to handle and takes away some of the energy you need for the game."

above: Frik du Preez and Albie Bates (Northern Transvaal) tackle Chris Laidlaw (New Zealand)

above: Mark Cueto (England) and Alesana Tuilagi (Samoa) 133

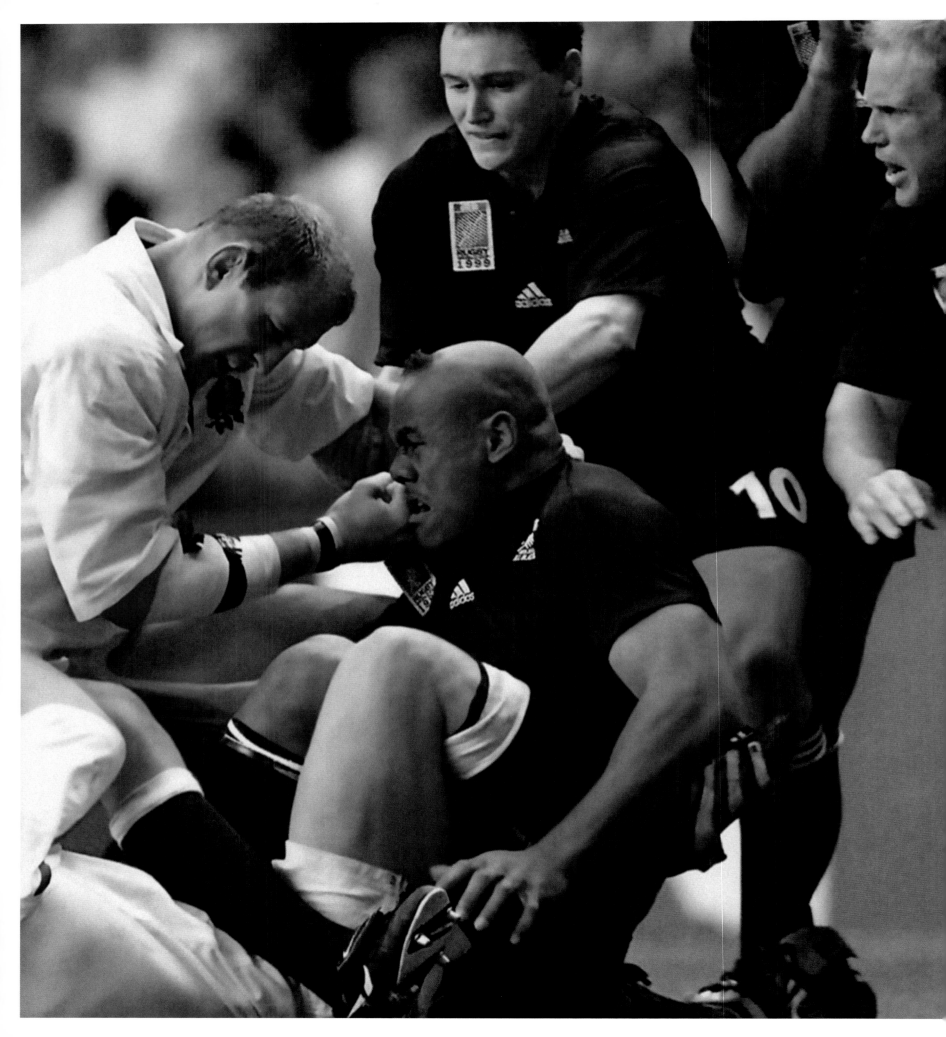

> "In my day, there was a weird sort of code of honour which said you could punch a guy in the face, but you couldn't kick him in the head."

JOHN KIRWAN

"I believe we got our approach wrong. We needed to be more expressive, to create more, but instead we played quite tactically and in a calculated manner rather than to our strengths. New Zealand was so organised and sharp that such an approach was never likely to succeed. It's always harder to defend against teams that take the initiative, create things and put pace on the game. In the second half, we had to defend and didn't do it very well. The images of the All Blacks scoring those tries are still in my head."

If anything, the semifinal loss to South Africa at a water-logged Kings Park in Durban at the 1995 World Cup was even harder to bear.

"Like most rugby players, we preferred to play with the sun shining from a blue sky. It was very difficult: kick-off was delayed twice because of the rain and we had to stay in the dressing-room drinking coffee and tea. It was quiet; the motivation was inside. It was almost dinner-time but of course we couldn't eat."

South Africa led 19–15 going into the last quarter but the momentum was with France. It seemed as if giant loose forward Abdelatif Benazzi had scored the winning try when he bodysurfed towards the line, but the referee ruled he'd been held up short. The resultant five-metre scrum was reset four times as the French pack strove for a pushover try, but the Springboks held on.

"It was very tough to come that close to making the World Cup final, but that's sport," says Sella. "That's a page you must turn. Some found that difficult; some of our players and management could not accept this defeat. I was very disappointed that night; I couldn't sleep. I got up at six to go for a jog and met several team-mates doing the same thing – it was a good way to clear the head. At training that afternoon our coach Pierre Berbizier gave us a soccer ball. It was much better to see smiles than the atmosphere earlier, which was as if someone had died. That's not sport."

The third place play-off game, in which France defeated England 19–9, was Sella's 111th and last game for his country.

Martin Johnson, who also played in that game, believes dwelling on the significance of the occasion and therefore the consequences of defeat only increases the fear of failure, which is such a big part of top-level sport: "You're taking part in high-profile games with a lot of media scrutiny, so there's no hiding place," he says. "Everybody wants to talk to you about it. You know these really big games are going to be talked about for years to come, so you won't be able just to walk away and forget about it when the final whistle blows. If you care about it, you desperately want to win, so if you lose you're going to be dealing with that for a long time to come."

And when the game is seen to turn on a single incident, a single mistake, defeat can be sheeted home to an individual who, as Johnson points out, may have to live with that memory and the constant reminders for the rest of his career and beyond.

In *The Gold and the Black*, his history of the All Black–Wallaby rivalry, noted rugby writer Spiro Zavos analysed the photograph that dominated *The Sydney Morning Herald*'s front page the day after the 1994 Bledisloe Cup game at the Sydney Football Stadium, won by Australia 20–16.

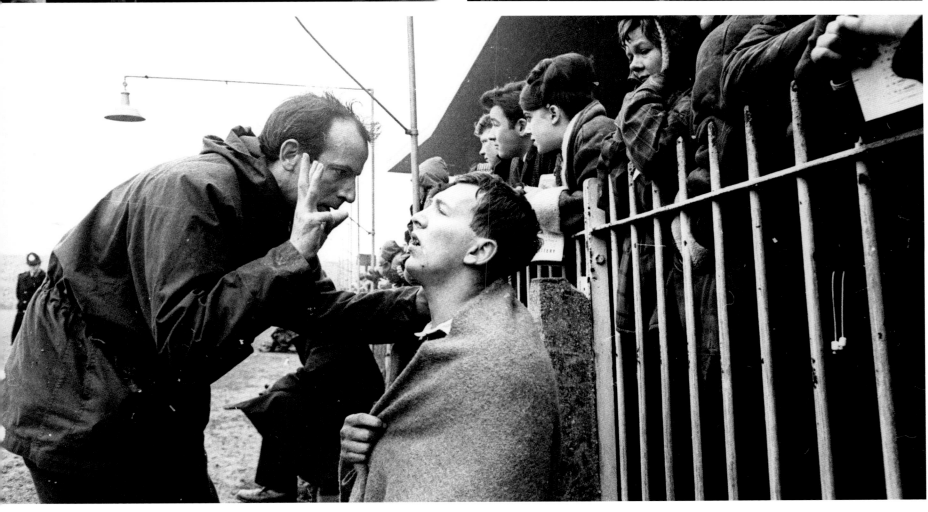

Sometimes there isn't just winning and losing in rugby – sometimes surviving is enough.

previous, top left: Wayne 'Buck' Shelford (New Zealand) previous, top right: Bobby Windsor (British Lions) and referee previous, bottom right: John Davies (Wales)

"The photograph shows a focused, calm-faced All Black winger Jeff Wilson," wrote Zavos, "his brain not yet registering the disaster that has happened to him, diving for the try-line with both feet off the ground, the force of the dive making his blond hair stand literally on end – and the ball is spilling centimetres away from his left hand. His right hand is stretched and tensing in what is an instinctive, unavailing grab to bring in the ball floating away from him like a fabulous, gleaming spheroid."

"[George] Gregan's arms encircle the waist of the All Black winger. And the ball is floating away... floating away, along with the marvellous tackle, into the collective memory of the thousands of people who are watching the test live and the millions seeing it on television. For every person involved, players and spectators, this moment frozen in the hundreds of black and white dots of a newspaper photograph will always be the infinity of 'Gregan's tackle'."

For Wilson, the pain of defeat was made infinitely worse by a section of the New Zealand public's refusal to let him forget his part in it. In his 2000 autobiography, *Seasons of Gold*, he revealed that he'd been living through his own private Groundhog Day:

"I don't need reminding that if I'd scored we would have won the game," he wrote. "I've been reminded of it almost every single week since and nothing in sport galls me more. Do people talk about how the All Blacks came back? No. Do people talk about how I beat three or four defenders to even get to the line? No. Do people ask how I scored this try or that try? No. All they can talk about, it seems, is how I was almost over the line when George Gregan pulled off a tackle of a lifetime and the ball shot forward out of my hands. That's the nature of sport. You win some, you lose some; the All Blacks win more than most."

"You're taking part in high-profile games with a lot of media scrutiny, so there's no hiding place. Everybody wants to talk to you about it. You know these really big games are going to be talked about for years to come, so you won't be able just to walk away and forget about it, when the final whistle blows. If you care about it you desperately want to win, so if you lose you're going to be dealing with that for a long time to come."

MARTIN JOHNSON

above: Justin Harrison (Australia) and Will Greenwood (England)

above: A disconsolate Sébastien Chabal (France) after losing to England in the semifinal of the Rugby World Cup   143

"But what am I constantly, repetitively, boringly reminded about and asked about? That tackle. I'm utterly sick of it. In answer to all those ghouls who like to live their lives on the black side of life: yes, I was devastated by not scoring. Wouldn't anyone be? Yes, I was upset. What the hell would they expect? That I danced for joy?"

"New Zealanders dwell too much on the bad times. They feel miserable when the All Blacks lose – and we had too much graphic evidence of that after the 1999 World Cup – and it's as if they want to know if the players feel miserable too. No, we feel a hell of a lot worse."

The protagonists went on to have stellar careers, but neither was able to escape from the giant shadow cast by that tackle. In a striking example of the Law of Unforeseen Consequences, Gregan would later admit to Wilson that his match-winning tackle became a millstone around his neck.

"He feels, like me, that it was one of the worst moments in his life, even though the result was good for his side," wrote Wilson. "He's now expected to make tackles like that all the time and, when he doesn't, he's asked why not."

right: The Irish team after losing to the All Blacks next: David Humphreys (Ireland)

Passion has many faces and takes many forms.

There's the passion of the fan: the crowd at the Millennium Stadium in Cardiff singing *Mae Hen Wlad Fy Nhadau* (Land of My Fathers) in one mighty, stirring voice; the supporters who follow their teams in the good times and bad, in fair weather and foul, across country lines, borders, even oceans; the volunteers who give their time to the game.

PASSION

"The surge of elation, the roar of the crowd, the back-slaps and high-fives: is there a greater thrill in rugby than scoring a try?"

PAUL THOMAS

There's the passion of the coach, from the teachers and dads who drum into youngsters the message that 14 players working together can create an opportunity for the fifteenth, all the way up to the men at the top of their professions who sit or stand or prowl in coaches' boxes high above the world's great grounds, hoping their players can see what they see.

There's the passion of the team which can reveal itself in a bloody-minded refusal to yield or in scorning the percentage play in favour of a surge of imagination and daring.

But it always comes from within; it always derives from love.

"Passion means... not dying wondering how good you and the team could be."

NICK FARR-JONES

To Nick Farr-Jones, passion means "getting out of bed in the morning with your feet spinning. It means being prepared to do the hard yards: blood, sweat and tears; squeezing every last drop from the lemon. It means not dying wondering how good you and the team could be. You've got to love what you do."

John Kirwan is often asked why he, as a New Zealander, is so passionate about coaching Japan: "I don't really know how to answer that except to say that I really love rugby, and when I commit to something, I do so with everything I've got. I've got a great desire for other people to experience the life I did. I want these players to look back at the end of their careers and think: 'That was the greatest time of my life; it moulded me as a person and made me a better man'."

"When we beat Samoa in Apia in 2010, I was so proud of the players I seriously thought I was going to cry – I had a tear in my eye when I was giving them a hug in the changing room. We'd been driving towards being a special team and talking about getting that big win and this was it. They didn't just beat Samoa, they outplayed them across the park, showed incredible courage, tackled till they couldn't tackle any more.

"For me, passion is committing to something you love. I don't think I could do anything without it."

For Martin Johnson, playing with passion means using the emotion generated by the occasion to perform better: "We see it every year: teams somehow get themselves up to beat more talented opponents. There's this perception that top-class sportsmen are cold, calculating, self-absorbed individuals, but the beauty of sport is that it matters to a lot of people. It's about tapping into that and feeding off it to play well for your club or your country, for your team-mates and supporters."

"Genius," said the inventor Thomas Edison, "is one per cent inspiration and 99 per cent perspiration." A similar sentiment, credited by some to Hollywood mogul Sam Goldwyn and by others to American founding father Thomas Jefferson, is that "the harder I work, the luckier I get".

The message is that, if you want to get to the top and achieve great things, you've got to go the extra mile. What drives individuals to put in those lonely hours? Ambition can provide a spur but the best motivation is having a passion for what you do.

Johnson: "Passion is playing the game with emotion and a need to succeed and be the best. It means training every day to be the best player you can be. People judge you on what happens out on the big stage, but you have to want to work hard when you're young and doing it for no reward or recognition; you're doing it because you want to."

Farr-Jones doubts that you can make it to the top in rugby without passion. "To survive and succeed at international level requires extreme commitment and you won't commit without passion. The best players I played with were the most disciplined, committed and passionate. They were always the hardest workers."

Every young rugby player is told that the surest way to get hurt is to go into contact tentatively, self-protectively. Sometimes it's put the other way around: if you go in hard, the other guy will feel it more than you will. What enables players to go into battle with no fear? The answer, once again, is passion.

"There are very few people like Buck Shelford who actually thrive on physical contact," says Kirwan, "most of us have to get ourselves up for it. Richie McCaw goes onto the field knowing that every time he goes in after the ball at the breakdown, a couple of 120-kilogram locks are going to try to take his head off. Do people really believe he's doing it for the money? Do they really think he doesn't have a passion for it?"

Farr-Jones makes the interesting observation that even though passion is a necessity in some positions, in others it needs to be controlled. "The optimum arousal for tight forwards, halfbacks and wings may be different. The big guys who work in the dark places need to get aroused, but if you're in the inside back positions that get first use of the ball, you don't want to get too aroused."

All rugby players at the top level are passionate but some are more passionate than others. These ultra-passionate individuals are enormously valuable to a team when their enthusiasm rubs off on, and inspires others. But if they can't control their passion, they may become a liability.

What enables players to go into battle with no fear? The answer, once again, is passion.

"The game is more strictly policed than in the days before the all-seeing eye of television and assistant referees and citing and disciplinary procedures," says Joel Stransky. "But the core elements and principles haven't changed: you play as strongly and robustly as you can within the laws of the game but, if you cross that line, there are consequences. It's a matter of knowing where the line is. Bakkies Botha is a very passionate player but there have been times when his passion has caused him to cross the line and let his team down."

It's sometimes argued that there's less passion in the game since it went professional. The argument seems to be that players are now primarily motivated by money rather than by national pride or pride in the jersey. Those making the charge that the contemporary player doesn't care enough seem to have forgotten that part of the ethos of amateurism was that one shouldn't care too much.

Amateurism in its pure, ideological form was a class-based concept in which one essentially played for fun and it was therefore ungentlemanly, if not downright unsporting, to take it too seriously. When, in 1947, cricket batsman Denis Compton broke Jack Hobbs' records for centuries in an English season, an agitated admirer wrote to a cricket writer seeking reassurance: "I hardly expected Compton to score 18 hundreds in a season. I thought him too good a player for that sort of thing. Am I right in assuming that Denis played his usual cricket and the 18 hundreds just happened in the process?"

In *Kings of Rugby*, his marvellous account of the 1959 British Lions' tour of Australia and New Zealand, Terry McLean related how in the game against Wairarapa Bush, with the raw-boned locals hot on attack, the Irish centre David Hewitt wandered over to his wing Tony O'Reilly and said, "You know, Tony, I wish

I had my camera with me – there are some lovely views around here. I think I'll come back afterwards to take some shots."

McLean observed that "the last such statement by an All Black centre under similar circumstances was made in 1822".

"I understand what the older generation are saying," says Johnson, "and we have to listen to them – it's still a game of rugby; you're still a member of a team. But there are different influences on players today. It's their job to be at the training ground ready to work, but you have to have passion because it can be difficult. Once you start to watch the clock, that's not rugby."

After the All Blacks were hammered by the Wallabies 28–7 at Stadium Australia in 1999, Andrew Mehrtens declared that "we were out-passioned", adding a new term to the rugby lexicon. That went some way towards explaining the 40-point turnaround – a month earlier, the All Blacks had beaten the Wallabies 34–15 at Eden Park – but it also raised the question that has flummoxed fans, players and particularly coaches for many decades: why do teams play passionately one week and not the next?

As England manager, Johnson has an intense interest in this enduring mystery. "That's part of the challenge of dealing with a team of 22 individuals and the wider squad. What lifts them to produce a good performance? Some of it comes from within, some of it is external. We've all seen teams that have come off a bad loss and been written off by the public and media turn around and produce a big performance because it's a basic human drive to come out fighting when you're cornered. The most difficult thing is to find a formula that works for individuals and the collective because it's so hard to put your finger on."

154   *above: Rob Howley (Wales) dives to score a try*

"You see it in games: a team gets behind, they're struggling, then suddenly it turns around. Perhaps it's because the leaders stepped up or an individual did something to lift the rest of the team. We'd all love to know how to switch it on and off. The French have perhaps the biggest differential between good and bad in terms of emotion. When they're up, they're almost unplayable but, when they're flat, they're a very different animal. Anglo-Saxons are mentally a bit more consistent, so you don't have those big drop-offs in emotion."

Stransky reckons that if anyone can come up with the answer, he or she will make a fortune. "It's a strange thing. No player consciously plays with less passion this week than he did last week. Home advantage seems to be a big factor – the Irish in Ireland are like men possessed. Then again, a team can go out full of passion but a loose pass or an intercept try can make the passion drain away like water out of a whirlpool. A team may be flat but an inspirational half-time speech can transform them. It seems to be something deep down inside and some teams appear to have the knack of getting up for big games. A lot of it's down to leadership – understanding the mood in the group and knowing which strings to pull."

Kirwan doesn't think it's all that mysterious. As far as he's concerned, it simply reflects the fact that rugby players aren't machines. "Do normal people go to work with the same level of commitment every day? Some days you over-prepare and you're flat; other days the opposition is more aggressive than you – it doesn't mean you're not trying. You can be so hyped up, you can't sleep the night before. It's such a mind game. The thing about being a normal person is that you can drive to work thinking about all sorts of things, have a coffee, have a chat, spend an hour getting down to work. In our game, if you're not prepared when the whistle blows, you're going to be exposed in the next two minutes."

158   *above: The Fijian team perform their cibi   right: Israel Dagg and Mils Muliaina (New Zealand)   next: The All Blacks perform the haka*

"Saturday afternoon in the Western Highlands and I find myself lying in a corner of the Mushroom Field, seeped in the damp of the Oban-to-Crinan canal. My cheek and eye are crushed into mud, several half-naked strangers are piled on top of me and softly, from the sea-grey sky, it starts to rain. Which is when I think: 'God, I love this game'."

RICHARD BEARD

"The women sit, getting colder and colder, on a seat getting harder and harder, watching oafs, getting muddier and muddier."

VIRGINIA GRAHAM

above: New Zealand and British Lions match at Athletic Park, Wellington   right: Curtain-raiser at Newlands Stadium, Cape Town

"The beauty of sport is that it matters to a lot of people. It's about tapping into that and feeding off it to play well for your club or your country, for your team-mates and supporters."

MARTIN JOHNSON

168   *above, top: English fans celebrate with Prince William and Prince Harry   above, bottom: Brian Moore (England)*

"Rugby fans are all experts when it comes to knowing how the game should have been played and all believe they would make excellent coaches if someone would just give them a chance."

MARIANNE THAMM

"Handshakes all round, a bit of boozy banter and off home. Via the pub. My kind of sport. You don't boo the other team's kicker, you don't hurl abuse at the players, you don't boo the national anthem. You just enjoy the game and have a good singsong."

IAIN MACINTOSH

There is a saying, understandably popular in rugby circles, that rugby is a game for hooligans played by gentlemen while soccer is a game for gentlemen played by hooligans.

JottingsOnRugby.com, an Australian website devoted to rugby history, sought to establish who actually came up with this oft-quoted saying which over the years has been attributed to a range of people, including some notable literary figures.

It sounds like something Oscar Wilde might have said, but in fact he seems to have thought the opposite: his only recorded comment on the game was, "Rugby is a good occasion for keeping 30 bullies far from the centre of town".

HONOUR

"Rugby is a game for hooligans played by gentlemen while soccer is a game for gentlemen played by hooligans."

George Orwell is among the usual suspects when it comes to acerbic witticisms. Although Orwell didn't address rugby directly, there's no reason to think he saw it as an exception to this Orwellian rule: "Serious sport has nothing to do with fair play. It is bound up with hatred, jealousy, boastfulness, disregard of all rules and sadistic pleasure in witnessing violence. In other words, it is war minus the shooting."

It wasn't Rudyard Kipling either, although he did squeeze two memorable sporting images – "flannelled fools" and "muddied oafs" – into a single line of poetry.

The name William Percy Carpmael, the founder of the Barbarian Football Club, surfaces now and again, possibly because the saying has a faint echo of the Baa-Baas' motto: "Rugby football is a game for gentlemen of all classes, but for no bad sportsmen of any class."

> ## "The great honour is being out there on the stage setting an example for future players and leaders."

JOEL STRANSKY

One notable author and wit who seems to have slipped under the radar is PG Wodehouse, whose short story "The Ordeal of Young Tuppy" (from the 1930 collection *Very Good, Jeeves!*) revolves around a torrid game of rugby. In the hope of impressing a Miss Dalgleish ("one of those largish, corn-fed girls"), Bertie Wooster's chum, Tuppy Glossop, agrees to turn out for Upper Bleaching in the annual grudge match against the neighbouring village of Hockley-cum-Meston.

Bertie doesn't think this is a good idea: "Rugby football is a game I can't claim absolutely to understand in all its niceties, if you know what I mean. I can follow the broad, general principles, of course. I mean to say, I know that the main scheme is to work the ball down the field and somehow deposit it over the line. In order to squelch this programme, each side is allowed to put in a certain amount of assault and battery and do things to its fellow man which, if done elsewhere, would result in 14 days without the option coupled with some strong remarks from the bench."

The game unfolds according to Bertie's blueprint. And although Tuppy scores the winning try, he has little to show for allowing "a mob of homicidal maniacs to kick me in the ribs and stroll about on my face" since Miss Dalgleish chooses not to attend. But it wasn't Wodehouse, nor was it Welsh actor Richard Burton, a keen rugby fan, who summed up the game thus: "Rugby is a wonderful show – dance, opera and suddenly the blood of a killing."

JottingsOnRugby.com's dogged quest led to an article that appeared in *The Times* in 1953, which attributed the remark to an unnamed chancellor of Cambridge University. Asked to sum up a debate on the respective merits of rugby union and association football, the chancellor began by saying: "It's clear that one is a gentleman's game played by hooligans, and the other a hooligan's game played by gentlemen." Being a self-confessed sporting ignoramus, he left it to the audience to decide which was which.

The misquotation has entered popular usage because it contains a recognisable, enduring truth: since rugby allows its participants to engage in a level of physical violence, which, as Bertie Wooster pointed out, would qualify as an assault in any other setting, it therefore demands self-control, stoicism and a clear understanding of what is acceptable and what is unacceptable. This is rugby's code of honour.

Joel Stransky describes it as: "fronting up honestly in battle. You go out on the field, give your heart and soul, and come off battered, bruised and sometimes shattered."

As John Kirwan observes, the line separating the acceptable from the unacceptable has shifted over the years: "In my day, there was a weird sort of code of honour which said you could punch a guy in the face, but you couldn't kick him in the head. It sounds barbaric, but that's the way it was. It's different today: in some ways the game's more violent and aggressive, but if you take a

cheap shot and injure a guy, you could affect his livelihood. Today's code of honour is bound up with respect for your fellow professional."

What hasn't changed, however, is that the physical nature of rugby union is central to its ethos.

Kirwan says, "People sometimes say to me that they hope professional rugby doesn't end up like soccer. It will never end up like soccer because there's contact and, where there's contact, there's honesty. It will always be about honesty because if you don't have courage, you won't survive. Rugby is a game of fundamental honesty called contact."

Philippe Sella maintains that discipline is the key, not only to being successful but also to being true to the game's code. He looks back ruefully on the very few occasions on which he failed to live up to that code.

"When Les Bleus played the Wallabies at the Sydney Football Stadium in 1990, a fight started between Phil Kearns and our number nine. I was very far away but I went in to see what was happening as it really was quite a massive fight. I was standing between Peter FitzSimons and Abdelatif Benazzi when it flared up again, and I punched FitzSimons. Surprisingly, it was a very good punch and he ended up on the floor. They replayed the incident on the big screen and all I could see was me throwing the punch. It wasn't a glorious moment in my career. I wasn't proud because many players have been sent off for less."

"In the whole of my international career, I only punched two other players, both of them nice guys – Rob Andrew of England and Andrew Slack of Australia. In each instance they pulled my jersey when I was trying to get in support of the ball carrier who had broken the defence. It was something I didn't like at all."

"The Andrew incident happened in the quarterfinal of the 1991 World Cup. I didn't know it was Rob, who was a guy I appreciated a lot. As he pulled my jersey I twisted around and lashed out. Then I saw it was him on the floor and I was very sorry."

"Slack was the Wallaby captain when we played them in Sydney in 1986. In his speech after the match he said people might have seen an incident in which he'd been punched by Philippe Sella. Andrew admitted that he'd pulled my jersey. 'I made a mistake,' he said, 'he made a mistake, so it's one point each.' That's the rugby family."

Then there is the honour of representing one's country.

Nick Farr-Jones feels sorry for today's players. He believes they are missing out on the privileges that used to be part and parcel of international rugby, but have fallen by the wayside under professionalism. "Rugby opened all sorts of doors and gave me a passport to the world, great friendships and fantastic memories: all the fun and mateship of touring; the great dinners with the opposition; the privilege of pulling on the jersey and belting out the anthem.

"I suppose my generation were the last of the amateurs. I have no regrets about missing out on professionalism. First, I wanted to get a tertiary education and become a lawyer, and I'm not sure I'd have that opportunity today. Second, we got the chance to go on long tours which gave you a chance to get outside the team bubble and meet people and experience different cultures. Third, we played in the afternoon which meant that we had formal after-match dinners which was when you got to know your opponents – what the French call the *troisième mi-temps*, the third half. Now they play at night and, after the game, they go through this nonsense of ice baths and eating fruit and don't emerge from the dressing-room till 10.30. There's no reception, no breaking bread with the opposition."

If there were one incident in Farr-Jones' career which epitomised what he treasured about international rugby and fears may be lost to the game, it took place at Carisbrook, Dunedin, in 1993. With the outstanding Michael Lynagh unavailable, Queenslander Pat Howard was handed the number ten jersey for the one-off test against the All Blacks at the so-called House of Pain, a venue where Australia had never won.

It would have been a daunting assignment for an experienced player. For a 19-year-old debutant more suited to playing at inside centre and having to contend with the great All Blacks open-side flanker Michael Jones, it was mission impossible. Having been knocked out of the 1991 World Cup by the Wallabies and beaten 2–1 by them in a series the previous year, the All Blacks were out for blood, and the first item on the menu was the rookie fly-half.

"Pat was thrown in at the deep end and had a hard day," says Farr-Jones. "After the game I said to [All Black fly-half] Grant Fox: 'There's a young fellow over there who's hurting, can you have a word to him?' Sixty minutes later Foxy was still with him. I don't know if that happens these days."

England's Martin Johnson confirms that the after-match ain't what it used to be. "When I look back to how it was when I started playing, the Six Nations was more about the occasion. You'd play in Dublin or Paris and after the game you'd put on a suit and go to a dinner, have a few beers with the opposition, and then have a night of it. The next day you'd go home with a hangover and have a couple of days off. That doesn't really happen anymore because there's another big game coming up next weekend and you focus on recovery."

While representing one's country remains as great an honour as ever, Farr-Jones questions where it sits in player agents' scheme of things: "If I could change one thing about the game today, it would be the involvement of agents. I think they're parasitic on the players and advise their clients badly. Often that advice is to chase the dollar instead of the honour of representing your nation. I had an offer to go Cambridge University but I wanted to be part of a great Wallaby team."

"Rugby remains one of the great games, precisely because it totally involves the body, not just the feet, or a stick or a racquet. There are also qualities about the sport, like unselfishness and unpretentiousness, that distinguish it from flashier rivals."

DENIS WELCH

"Part of the All Black code of honour was be humble and make sure that, if you were going to talk the talk, you then went out and walked the walk."

JOHN KIRWAN

For Kirwan, representing his country was, quite simply, life-changing: "I got into the team as a young man and it really defined and moulded me. Part of the All Black code of honour was be humble and make sure that, if you were going to talk the talk, you then went out and walked the walk. If you made a commitment to the team, if you promised you were going to do this or do that but you didn't back it up, you didn't last. And you looked at yourself in the mirror before you went around questioning other people. If you'd played well and done your job, then you could criticise someone else – but not before."

"It was a privilege and an honour to be an All Black. I'm a butcher from Mangere Bridge who lives in Venice and works in Tokyo and probably earns more than the Prime Minister. I only got where I am because of the All Blacks."

And Stransky makes the important point that the honour of representing one's country comes with a responsibility to future generations and the wider game. "The great honour is being out there on the stage setting an example for future players and leaders. The aim should be to walk away at the end of your career knowing you've set high standards and played hard but fair."

"When played by the best exponents of the game on earth, rugby union satisfies the soul like nothing else."

GREG GROWDEN

previous: Bob Davidson (Australia) is carried from the field by Barbarians players   right: Sébastien Chabal (France)   next: English players take a break

INFORMATION

IMAGES

Page 2–3	1960	A young rugby player scores a try during a local final.
Page 8	July 1998, South Africa	Deserted rugby field.
Page 11	Circa 1980	French rugby international Jean-Pierre Rives.
Page 12–13	June 2008, New Zealand	All Black Richie McCaw signs autographs for fans during a training session and press conference at Rugby Park, Christchurch.
Page 15	November 1984, Ireland	Wallaby Nick Farr-Jones passes the ball in a match against Ireland at Lansdowne Road, Dublin.
Page 16–17	June 1995, South Africa	Francois Pienaar of South Africa and team celebrate after the Rugby World Cup final against the All Blacks at Ellis Park, Johannesburg.
Page 18	October 1999, England	All Black Jonah Lomu plays against Tonga at Ashton Gate Stadium, Bristol.
Page 20–21	July 2010, New Zealand	All Black Tom Donnelly competes with Springbok Victor Matfield in the lineout during the Tri-Nations match at Eden Park, Auckland.
Page 23	1995, South Africa	Springbok Joel Stransky during a Rugby World Cup match.
Page 24–25	20 June 1987, New Zealand	All Black John Kirwan is tackled by French players Patrice Lagisquet (11) and Franck Mesnel (10).
Page 26	June 2003, New Zealand	All Black Tana Umaga rolls Colin Charvis of Wales into the recovery position at Waikato Stadium, Hamilton.
Page 27	July 1980, South Africa	Hugo Porta of Argentina plays for the South African Barbarians during a match against the British Lions at Kings Park Stadium, Durban.
Page 28–29	March 1989, France	Philippe Sella of France opposes (L to R) Scott Hastings, Derek White and Peter Dods of Scotland during the Five-Nations match at Parc des Princes, Paris.
Page 30		Sean Fitzpatrick (New Zealand).
Page 31	March 2009, England	France's Sébastien Chabal rests after an England try during their Six-Nations match at Twickenham Stadium, London.
Page 32	November 2003, Australia	England's Martin Johnson is tackled during the Rugby World Cup final against Australia at Telstra Stadium, Sydney.
Page 34	June 1995, South Africa	South African President Nelson Mandela congratulates Springbok captain, Francois Pienaar, after South Africa won the Rugby World Cup final against New Zealand at Ellis Park, Johannesburg.
Page 35 (top)	March 1955	An Irish player signs autographs after a match against Scotland.
Page 35 (bottom)	July 1974, South Africa	Andy Irvine (British Lions) shakes hands with a Leopards player after a match in East London, Eastern Cape.
Page 37	November 2005, England	Tana Umaga and Jerry Collins of New Zealand during the national anthems prior to a match between England and New Zealand at Twickenham Stadium, London.
Page 38–39	November 1967, France	The All Blacks perform the haka before the match against France at Colombes Stadium, Paris.
Page 40–41	September 2005, New Zealand	A Wallaby supporter sings the New Zealand national anthem prior to a Tri-Nations rugby clash between Australia and the All Blacks at Eden Park, Auckland.
Page 42	February 2009	Marco Bortolami and Mauro Bergamasco sing the Italian anthem during a Six-Nations match against England.
Page 44–45	March 2005, England	England's Matt Stevens and Steve Thompson sing the national anthem before a Six-Nations match against Italy at Twickenham Stadium, London.
Page 46–47	South Africa	Springboks Bob Skinstad and Joe van Niekerk sing the national anthem before a test at Ellis Park, Johannesburg.
Page 49	September 2008, Australia	All Black Daniel Carter scores a try against Australia in a Tri-Nations rugby match at Suncorp Stadium, Brisbane.
Page 50–51	October 2007, France	Springbok winger Bryan Habana scores the last try of the match during the Rugby World Cup semifinal against Argentina at the Stade de France, Saint-Denis, Paris.
Page 53	November 2003, Australia	England captain Martin Johnson celebrates with the Webb Ellis Cup after winning the Rugby World Cup final against Australia at Telstra Stadium, Sydney.
Page 54	November 2009, Ireland	Australian winger Drew Mitchell celebrates the opening try during the match against Ireland at Croke Park, Dublin.
Page 55	Circa 1981, Wales	Welshman John Peter Rhys 'JPR' Williams is chaired off the pitch at a match against England at Cardiff Arms Park.
Page 56	September 2009, Australia	Wallaby Adam Ashley-Cooper celebrates with fans after scoring a try during the Tri-Nations match against South Africa at Suncorp Stadium, Brisbane.
Page 57 (top)	September 2008, Australia	Wallaby Adam Ashley-Cooper dives in to score a try during the Tri-Nations Bledisloe Cup match against New Zealand at Suncorp Stadium, Brisbane.
Page 57 (bottom)	November 2003, Australia	Wallaby Phil Waugh hugs supporters after Australia won the Rugby World Cup semifinal against New Zealand at Telstra Stadium, Sydney.
Page 58–59	November 2009, England	All Black Mils Muliaina dives over the try-line but the try is disallowed during the Investec Challenge Series match against England at Twickenham Stadium, London.
Page 60	October 1999, England	Richard Dourthe of France celebrates the French victory over New Zealand in the Rugby World Cup semifinal at Twickenham Stadium, London.
Page 61 (top)	June 1987, New Zealand	All Black captain David Kirk kisses the Webb Ellis Cup after the Rugby World Cup final between New Zealand and France at Eden Park, Auckland.
Page 61 (bottom)	November 2003, Australia	England's Jason Robinson celebrates winning the Rugby World Cup final against Australia at Telstra Stadium, Sydney.
Page 62	August 2003, New Zealand	The All Blacks celebrate winning the Tri-Nations second Bledisloe Cup match against Australia at Eden Park, Auckland.
Page 63	November 2005, Ireland	Ireland's Johnny O'Connor scores a try against Romania at Lansdowne Road, Dublin.
Page 64–65	November 1999, Wales	Wallaby John Eales (centre) celebrates with team-mates after winning the Rugby World Cup final against France at Millennium Stadium, Cardiff.

Page 66–67	November 2008, England	The Springboks celebrate during an Investec Challenge Series match against England at Twickenham Stadium, London.
Page 69	October 2007, France	England's Andrew Sheridan and Wallaby Matt Dunning clash during the quarterfinal of the Rugby World Cup at Stade Vélodrome, Marseille.
Page 70–71	February 1994	Muddy players Richard Cockerill and Martin Johnson fight for the ball in a match between Bath and Leicester.
Page 72	July 1968, New Zealand	All Black Colin Meads gets a hand to the ball ahead of France's Benoît Dauga in the second test at Athletic Park, Wellington.
Page 72 (right)	March 1983	Flanker Jean-Pierre Rives shows some battle scars in a Five-Nations match against Wales.
Page 75	September 2006, South Africa	All Black captain Richie McCaw, leaves the field battered and bruised following his team's loss in the Tri-Nations test match against South Africa at Royal Bafokeng Stadium, Rustenburg.
Page 76	June 2008, England	Barbarian's Australian player Stephen Larkham grabs England's Captain Nick Easter after Easter scored a try during their Gartmore Challenge match at Twickenham, London.
Page 77	1978, Scotland	All Blacks captain Graham Mourie about to receive stitches.
Page 78	October 2007, Wales	Yannick Jauzion of France tackles All Black Luke McAlister during the quarterfinal of the Rugby World Cup at Millennium Stadium, Cardiff.
Page 79	October 2001, Ireland	Keith Wood of Ireland is stopped by Jason Leonard and Richard Hill of England during the Six-Nations match at Lansdowne Road, Dublin.
Page 80	October 2007, France	England's fly-half Jonny Wilkinson and Springbok hooker and captain John Smit clash during the Rugby World Cup final at Stade de France, Saint-Denis, Paris.
Page 81	November 2003, Australia	George Gregan of Australia and Keith Wood of Ireland clash during the Rugby World Cup Pool A match at Telstra Dome, Melbourne.
Page 82–83	June 2003, New Zealand	All Black Tana Umaga is grabbed by English player Lawrence Dallaglio during a match at Westpac Stadium, Wellington.
Page 84	October 1999, Ireland	Wallaby Tim Horan tackles Justin Bishop of Ireland during the Rugby World Cup Pool E match at Lansdowne Road, Dublin.
Page 85	June 2006, Australia	Stirling Mortlock of the Wallabies makes a break during a Cook Cup match against England at Telstra Stadium, Sydney.
Page 86		Mud and guts.
Page 87	May 2001, Australia	England's Shelley Rae is held off by the Australian defence during a women's rugby match at Waratah Park, Sydney.
Page 88–89	November 2003, Australia	The head of French captain Yannick Bru peers out of a scrum during the Rugby World Cup third place play-off against New Zealand.
Page 91	October 2007, France	John Philip 'Bakkies' Botha of South Africa is trapped at the bottom of a maul during the Rugby World Cup final against England at Stade de France, Saint-Denis, Paris.
Page 92	November 2004, Scotland	Wallaby George Smith finds himself crushed in a ruck during a friendly match against Scotland at Hampden Park, Glasgow.
Page 93	October 1999, England	Springbok Os du Randt barges Wallaby George Gregan during the Rugby World Cup match at Twickenham Stadium, London.
Page 95	October 2007, France	Springbok Schalk Burger is tackled by Akapusi Qera (L) and Vilimoni Delasau of Fiji during the quarterfinal of the Rugby World Cup at Stade Vélodrome, Marseille.
Page 96–97	March 2007, England	Christophe Dominici of France tackles England's Shane Geraghty during a Six-Nations match at Twickenham Stadium, London.
Page 99	1999, Wales	Welsh players (L to R) Peter Rogers, Garin Jenkins, Shane Howarth, Chris Wyatt and Brett Sinkinson celebrate their win against South Africa at Millennium Stadium, Cardiff.
Page 100–01	October 2007, France	Springbok hooker and captain John Smit holds the William Webb Ellis Cup as South African President Thabo Mbeki (L) and team-mates celebrate winning the Rugby World Cup final against England at Stade de France, Saint-Denis, Paris.
Page 102–03	October 2003, Australia	Ireland's Malcolm O'Kelly, Peter Stringer and Alan Quinlan about to play Argentina in the Rugby World Cup at the Adelaide Oval.
Page 104	South Africa	South African police officer Elroy 'Bumper' Gouws plays rugby at De Rust, near Oudtshoorn.
Page 106	October 1999, England	The France team celebrate after beating New Zealand to win the semifinal match of the Rugby World Cup played at Twickenham Stadium, London.
Page 107	November 2010, France	French lock Julien Pierre prepares before a scrum during the Autumn International match against Fiji at Stade de la Beaujoire, Nantes.
Page 108	October 1999, France	England's Lawrence Dallaglio in action during the Rugby World Cup quarterfinal match against South Africa at Stade de France, Saint-Denis, Paris.
Page 109	February 1999, England	Ireland and Wales players tussle for the ball during a Five-Nations match at Wembley Stadium, London.
Page 110–11	February 2010, Wales	Ryan Jones of Wales grabs the ball in a lineout as Julien Bonnaire of France falls down during a Six-Nations match at Millennium Stadium, Cardiff.
Page 112	June 1995, South Africa	All Black winger Jonah Lomu runs through England fullback Mike Catt during the Rugby World Cup semifinal at Newlands Stadium, Cape Town.
Page 115	March 2003, England	Try-scorer Josh Lewsey of England is congratulated by team-mate Lawrence Dallaglio during a Six-Nations match against Italy at Twickenham Stadium, London.
Page 116	March 2010, France	Sébastien Chabal of France celebrates with team-mates after winning the Six-Nations final against England at the Stade de France, Saint-Denis, Paris.
Page 117 (top)	1956, New Zealand	Springbok lock Chris de Nysschen remodels a hotel bed.
Page 117 (bottom left)	1952, England	Players relax in the baths after a match at Esher Rugby Club.
Page 117 (bottom right)	2002, Ireland	Keith Wood, Peter Clohessy and Brian O'Driscoll (L-R) of Ireland have a laugh on the way to training.
Page 118–19	August 2007	Ireland's John Hayes sees the funny side of Shane Horgan having his photo taken.

Page 120	2002, Ireland	David Wallace of Ireland receives a massage prior to a game.
Page 121	November 2010, Wales	The All Blacks celebrate their win following a match with Wales at Millennium Stadium, Cardiff.
Page 122	October 2007, France	Juan Martin Fernandez Lobbe (L) and Juan Manuel Leguizamon of Argentina celebrate winning the bronze final in the Rugby World Cup against France at Parc des Princes, Paris.
Page 123 (top)	October 2007, France	Puma Juan Manuel Leguizamon celebrates winning the bronze final in the Rugby World Cup against France at Parc des Princes, Paris.
Page 123 (bottom)	February 2005, France	French flanker Serge Betsen hugs scrum-half Dimitri Yachvili after he scored a try during the Six-Nations match against Wales at Stade de France, Saint-Denis, Paris.
Page 125	South Africa	Springbok and Northern Transvaal prop Mof Myburgh at a game against Western Province.
Page 126	November 2006, Ireland	Clontarf's Philip Perdue during a match against Shannon in Dublin.
Page 128–29	March 2010, Ireland	Jamie Roberts of Wales and Brian O'Driscoll of Ireland during a Six-Nations match at Croke Park, Dublin.
Page 130		A match between England and Italy.
Page 132	September 1970, South Africa	Northern Transvaal's Frik du Preez and Albie Bates tackle All Black Chris Laidlaw at Loftus Versfeld Stadium, Pretoria.
Page 133	26 November 2005, England	England's Mark Cueto is up-ended by Alesana Tuilagi of Samoa, which resulted in him being sent off during the Investec Challenge Series match at Twickenham Stadium, London.
Page 134	October 1999, England	England's Lawrence Dallaglio confronts All Blacks Jonah Lomu and Andrew Mehrtens at Twickenham Stadium, London.
Page 136	July 2008, New Zealand	Springbok Gurthrö Steenkamp after the Tri-Nations match against New Zealand at Carisbrook Stadium, Dunedin.
Page 137 (top left)	August 1988, Australia	Victorious All Black Captain Wayne Shelford leaves Concord Oval, Sydney.
Page 137 (top right)	June 1977, New Zealand	Bobby Windsor of the British Lions removes mud from the eye of referee G Harrison during a match against West Coast–Buller in Westport.
Page 137 (bottom)	March 1965, Wales	Welshman John Davies has his eyes checked after action on the field during a match against Ireland in Cardiff.
Page 138	June 2006, South Africa	Jean de Villiers screams after being injured during the first test match against Scotland at the Kings Park Stadium, Durban.
Page 139	June 2007, New Zealand	Sébastien Chabal of France lies in pain on the field during the first test against New Zealand at Eden Park, Auckland.
Page 140	November 2009, Scotland	Alex Grove and Nic de Luca of Scotland celebrate as Matt Giteau of Australia reacts to his missed conversion during a match at Murrayfield, Edinburgh.
Page 141	October 2007, Wales	A dejected Richie McCaw of New Zealand attends the post-match press conference after the quarterfinal of the Rugby World Cup at Millennium Stadium, Cardiff.
Page 142	November 2003, Australia	English centre Will Greenwood (bottom) reacts after winning the Rugby World Cup while Wallaby lock Justin Harrison looks dejected at Sydney Olympic Park.
Page 143	October 2007, France	Sébastien Chabal of France bows his head after losing to England in the semifinal of the Rugby World Cup 2007 at the Stade de France, Saint-Denis, Paris.
Page 144–45	November 2001, Ireland	The Ireland team after their defeat to New Zealand at Lansdowne Road, Dublin.
Page 146–47	February 2000, Ireland	Ireland's David Humphreys scores a try against Scotland in the Six-Nations match in Lansdowne Road, Dublin.
Page 149	June 1987, Australia	Serge Blanco of France scores the winning try against Australia in the Rugby World Cup semifinal at Concord Oval, Sydney.
Page 150	November 2003, Australia	Springbok Joost van der Westhuizen disputes the referee's decision during the Rugby World Cup Pool C match against Samoa at Suncorp Stadium, Brisbane.
Page 152–53	February 2010, France	Paul O'Connell of Ireland in action against France in the Six Nations at Stade de France, Saint-Denis, Paris.
Page 154	October 1999, Wales	Welsh scrum-half and captain Rob Howley dives to score a try during the Rugby World Cup first-round match between Wales and Japan at Millennium Stadium, Cardiff.
Page 155	October 2007, France	England's Joe Worsley celebrates the win against Australia in front of George Gregan in the quarterfinals of the Rugby World Cup at Stade Vélodrome, Marseille.
Page 156–57	March 2011, Wales	Ireland captain Brian O'Driscoll appeals to referee Jonathan Kaplan of South Africa after Mike Phillips of Wales scores a try in the corner during a Six-Nations match at Millennium Stadium, Cardiff.
Page 158	November 2004, Fiji	Fiji team performs their cibi at Churchill Park, Lautoka.
Page 159	August 2010, South Africa	All Blacks Israel Dagg and Mils Muliaina celebrate after Dagg scores the winning try in the Tri-Nations match against South Africa at the First National Bank Stadium, Johannesburg.
Page 160–61	October 2007, Wales	The All Blacks perform the haka in front of the French team before the quarterfinal of the Rugby World Cup at Millennium Stadium, Cardiff.
Page 162	July 1977, New Zealand	Lions forward Fran Cotton plays the New Zealand Juniors at Athletic Park, Wellington.
Page 164	June 1977, New Zealand	A view of a match between New Zealand and the British Lions in Wellington.
Page 165	1974, South Africa	Western Province rugby officials allow a curtain-raiser to be played before the British Lions and Southern Universities took to a muddy and rain-drenched Newlands Stadium, Cape Town.
Page 166	June 1995, South Africa	Scotland captain Gavin Hastings is chaired off the pitch after his final international in Pretoria, during the Rugby World Cup.
Page 167	October 2007, England	England fans watch the Rugby World Cup semifinal match against France on a giant screen at The O$_2$ arena, London.
Page 168 (top)	October 2007, France	Prince William and Prince Harry support England in the final of the Rugby World Cup against South Africa at Stade de France, Saint-Denis, Paris.

Page 168 (bottom)	1992	England hooker Brian Moore is lifted shoulder-high by the crowd as England wins the Five-Nations Grand Slam.
Page 169	1993	Darren Kellett of Manu Samoa is hoisted onto the shoulders of his fans after a Super-10 rugby union match.
Page 170–71	March 1995, England	England's Will Carling (centre) leads the England team on a lap of honour after winning the Grand Slam after the Five-Nations match against Scotland at Twickenham Stadium, London.
Page 172–73	June 2004, New Zealand	All Black fullback Mils Muliaina is hugged by a fan during a training session at Waitemata Park, Auckland.
Page 174	1980, France	French commentators Roger Couderc (left) and Pierre Albaladejo in Paris.
Page 175	November 1954, England	Rugby fans watching Oldham versus Rochdale.
Page 176	November 2003, Australia	An England fan in the crowd during the Rugby World Cup final between England and Australia at Telstra Stadium, Sydney.
Page 177	June 1976, England	A streaker is arrested during the Five-Nations match between England and Wales at Twickenham Stadium, London.
Page 178	March 2008, Scotland	An England fan kissing a Scotland fan at Murrayfield, Edinburgh.
Page 179	April 2009, Ireland	A Munster fan at a Heineken Cup quarterfinal.

Page 181	July 2009, South Africa	Springbok John Smit leads his team out before the third test match against the British and Irish Lions at Ellis Park, Johannesburg.
Page 182–83	August 2001, New Zealand	Three-year-old Timothy Sail greets All Black Jonah Lomu during an autograph session following a public training run at Victoria Park, Auckland.
Page 185	1990, France	Michael Jones stands during the New Zealand anthem before a match in France at the Parc des Princes, Paris.
Page 186	February 1985, England	Serge Blanco of France kicks as Rob Andrew of England tries to charge down during a match at Twickenham Stadium, London.
Page 188–89	November 2005, Scotland	Captain Tana Umaga of New Zealand is clapped off the field by the Scotland team following his team's win to complete the Grand Slam over the home unions at Murrayfield, Edinburgh.
Page 190–91	February 1958, Wales	Bob Davidson, captain of the Australian team, is carried off the field by opposing players after a match against the Barbarians at Cardiff Arms Park. Chatting to Davidson is Barbarians captain Cliff Morgan (second from left).
Page 193	September 2007, France	Sébastien Chabal of France is tackled by Felipe Contepomi of Argentina during the opening match of the Rugby World Cup 2007 at the Stade de France, Saint-Denis, Paris.
Page 194–95		A team of mud-covered English rugby players takes a break.

SELECT BIBLIOGRAPHY

Bush, Peter and Thomas, Paul, *A Life in Focus* (Hodder Moa, Auckland, 2009).

Fagan, Sean, 'Muddied Oafs of Rugby', www.JottingsOnRugby.com (blog entry 28 August 2010).

Freier, Adam, 'You can question Australia's form and ability, but not their ticker', www.rugbyheaven.com.au (article 8 August 2010).

Furst, Peter, *The Winning Edge: Champion Athletes on Life, Faith & Spirituality* (Grove House Publishing, Groombridge, 2000).

Hart, John and Thomas, Paul, *Straight from the Hart* (Hodder Moa Beckett, Auckland, 1996).

Johnson, Martin, *The Autobiography* (Headline, London, 2003).

Kirwan, John and Thomas, Paul, *Kirwan: Running on Instinct* (Moa, Auckland, 1992).

Lane, Christopher, ed., *A Century of Wisden* (A & C Black, London 2000).

McLean, Terry, *Kings of Rugby: the British Lions' 1959 Tour of New Zealand* (AH & AW Reed, Auckland, 1959).

Mulligan, Andrew, *All Blacks Tour 1963–64* (Souvenir Press, London, 1964).

Orwell, George, *Shooting an Elephant and Other Essays* (Secker & Warburg, London, 1950).

'The Evolution of Football', *The Times* (London, 30 January 1953).

Veysey, Alex, *Colin Meads: All Black* (Collins, Auckland, 1974).

Wilson, Jeff and Palenski, Ron, *Seasons of Gold* (Hodder Moa Beckett, Auckland, 2000).

Wodehouse, PG, 'The Ordeal of Young Tuppy', in *Very Good, Jeeves!* (Herbert Jenkins, London, 1958).

Zavos, Spiro, *The Gold and the Black: The Rugby Battles for the Bledisloe Cup* (Allen & Unwin, Sydney, 1995).

IMAGE CREDITS

Cover montage images used with permission of Getty Images and the individual copyright holders. Internal images used with permission of the following copyright holders: Page 2-3, Express/Getty Images; Page 8, Michel Birot; Page 11, Chris Smith/Hulton Archive/Getty Images; Page 12-13, Ross Land/Getty Images; Page 15, Bob Thomas/Getty Images; Page 16-17, Photosport; Page 18, Mark Leech/Offside; Page 20-21, Hannah Johnston/Getty Images; Page 23, Popperfoto/Getty Images; Page 24-25, Bob Thomas/Getty Images; Page 26, Ross Land/Getty Images; Page 27, Murrell/Allsport/Getty Images; Page 28-29, Bob Thomas/Getty Images; Page 30, Colorsport; Page 31, Eddie Keogh/Action Images; Page 32, Dave Rogers/Getty Images; Page 34, Dave Rogers/AFP/Getty Images; Page 35 (top), Malcolm Dunbar/Picture Post/Hulton Archive/Getty Images; Page 35 (bottom), Colin Elsey/Colorsport; Page 37, Ross Land/Getty Images; Page 38-39, Corbis; Page 40-41, New Zealand Herald/Kenny Rodger; Page 42, Mark Leech/Offside; Page 44-45, Richard Heathcote/Getty Images; Page 46-47, Wessel Oosthuizen; Page 49, Andrew Cornaga/Photosport; Page 50-51, William West/AFP/Getty Images; Page 53, Adam Pretty/Getty Images; Page 54, Stu Forster/Getty Images; Page 55, Colorsport; Page 56, Cameron Spencer/Getty Images; Page 57 (top), Ross Land/Getty Images; Page 57 (bottom), Stuart Hannagan/Getty Images; Page 58-59, Clive Rose/Getty Images; Page 60, Popperfoto/Getty Images; Page 61 (top), Georges Gobet/AFP/Getty Images; Page 61 (bottom), Dave Rogers/Getty Images; Page 62, Chris McGrath/Getty Images; Page 63, Lorraine O'Sullivan/INPHO; Page 64-65, Mike Hewitt/Allsport/Getty Images; Page 66-67, Jamie McDonald/Getty Images; Page 69, David Rogers/Getty Images; Page 70-71, Mark Leech/Offside; Page 72, Peter Bush/Colorsport; Page 72 (right), Offside/L'Equipe; Page 75, Ross Land/Getty Images; Page 76, Ian Kington/AFP/Getty Images; Page 77, Peter Bush/Photosport; Page 78, Ross Land/Getty Images; Page 79, Mike Hewitt/Allsport/Getty Images; Page 80, Martin Bureau/AFP/Getty Images; Page 81, Nick Laham/Getty Images; Page 82-83, Andrew Cornaga/Offside; Page 84, Nick Wilson/Allsport/Getty Images; Page 85, Cameron Spencer/Getty Images; Page 86, David Jacobs/Action Images; Page 87, Nick Laham/Allsport/Getty Images; Page 88-89, Tim Clayton; Page 91, Cameron Spencer/Getty Images; Page 92, Laurence Griffiths/Getty Images; Page 93, Dave Rogers/Allsport/Getty Images; Page 95, Julian Finney/Getty Images; Page 96-97, Warren Little/Getty Images; Page 99, Colin Elsey/Colorsport; Page 100-01, Martin Bureau/AFP/Getty Images; Page 102-03, Billy Stickland/INPHO; Page 104, Wessel Oosthuizen; Page 106, Alex Livesey/Allsport /Getty Images; Page 107, Franck Fife/AFP/Getty Images; Page 108, Clive Brunskill/Allsport/Getty Images; Page 109, Gary M Prior/Allsport/Getty Images; Page 110-11, Bertrand Langlois/AFP/Getty Images; Page 112, Vincent Amalvy/AFP/Getty Images; Page 115, Harry How/Getty Images; Page 116, Franck Fife/AFP/Getty Images; Page 117 (top), Wessel Oosthuizen; Page 117 (bottom left), Popperfoto/Getty Images; Page 117 (bottom right), INPHO/Billy Stickland; Page 118-19, Cathal Noonan/INPHO; Page 120, INPHO/Billy Stickland; Page 121, Phil Walter/Getty Images; Page 122, Cameron Spencer/Getty Images; Page 123 (top), Cameron Spencer/Getty Images; Page 123 (bottom), Damien Meyer/AFP/Getty Images; Page 125, Wessel Oosthuizen; Page 126, Morgan Treacy/INPHO; Page 128-29, Richard Heathcote/Getty Images; Page 130, Tom Jenkins/Guardian News & Media Ltd 2005; Page 132, Wessel Oosthuizen; Page 133, Phil Cole/Getty Images; Page 134, Offside/L'Equipe; Page 136, Brendon O'Hagan/AFP/Getty Images; Page 137 (top left), NZ Herald/APN; Page 137 (top right), Adrian Murrell/Getty Images; Page 137 (bottom), Martin Gilfeather/Express/Getty Images; Page 138, Touchline/Getty Images; Page 139, Phil Walter/Getty Images; Page 140, Jeff J Mitchell/Getty Images; Page 141, Andrew Cornaga/Photosport; Page 142, Christophe Simon/AFP/Getty Images; Page 143, Cameron Spencer/Getty Images; Page 144-45, INPHO/Billy Stickland; Page 146-47, INPHO/Patrick Bolger; Page 149, INPHO/Billy Stickland; Page 150, Jonathon Wood/Getty Images; Page 152-53, Andrew Coulridge/Action Images; Page 154, Patrick Kovarik/AFP/Getty Images; Page 155, Daily Mail; Page 156-57, Laurence Griffiths/Getty Images; Page 158, Andrew Cornaga/Photosport; Page 159, David Rogers/Getty Images; Page 160-61, Ross Land/AFP/Getty Images; Page 162, Colin Elsey/Colorsport; Page 164, Adrian Murrell/Getty Images; Page 165, Wessel Oosthuizen; Page 166, Simon Bruty/Getty Images; Page 167, Shaun Curry/AFP/Getty Images; Page 168 (top), Andy Hooper; Page 168 (bottom), David Davies/Offside; Page 169, Andrew Cornaga/Photosport; Page 170-71, Shaun Botterill/Allsport/Getty Images; Page 172-73, David Rogers/Getty Images; Page 174, Universal/TempSport/Corbis; Page 175, Bert Hardy/Picture Post/Getty Images; Page 176, Phil Walter/Getty Images; Page 177, Tony Duffy/Getty Images; Page 178, Lee Smith/Action Images; Page 179, INPHO/Dan Sheridan; Page 181, Duif du Toit/Gallo Images/Getty Images; Page 182-83, Ross Land/Getty Images; Page 185, Russell Cheyne/Allsport/Getty Images; Page 186, Mike Powell/Allsport/Getty Images; Page 188-89, Ross Land/Getty Images; Page 190-91, Popperfoto/Getty Images; Page 193, Laurence Griffiths/Getty Images; Page 194-95, Hulton Collection.

LITERARY PERMISSIONS

The publisher is grateful for literary permissions to reproduce the quotations appearing in this book subject to copyright. The publisher asserts that although quotations may be widely attributed to one author, it is not always possible to confirm the exact original source of a quotation. However the publisher acknowledges every effort has been made to trace the copyright holders, and apologises for any unintentional omission. We would be pleased to hear from any not acknowledged here and undertake to make all reasonable efforts to include the appropriate acknowledgement in any subsequent editions.

Pages 58 and 77— quotes from Simon Barnes reprinted by permission of *The Times* / NI Syndication; Page 152— quotations from *Kings of Rugby: the British Lions' 1959 Tour of New Zealand* reprinted by permission from Penguin Group (NZ); Page 163— from *Muddied Oafs: The Last Days of Rugger* by Richard Beard, published by Yellow Jersey Press. Reprinted by permission of The Random House Group Ltd; Page 179— quotation © Iain Macintosh, *Everything You Wanted To Know About Rugby But Were Too Afraid To Ask*, A&C Black Publishers Limited; Page 184— quotations from *Very Good, Jeeves!* By P G Wodehouse, published by Herbert Jenkins. Reprinted by permission of The Random House Group Ltd; Page 187— quotation from an editorial by Denis Welch in the *New Zealand Listener*, 22 May 1982. Reprinted by permission.

First edition published in 2011 by
Vision Sports Publishing Limited
19-23 High Street
Kingston upon Thames
Surrey
KT1 1LL
www.visionsp.co.uk

ISBN: 978-1907637-30-8

Produced and originated by PQ Blackwell Limited
116 Symonds Street, Auckland 1010, New Zealand
www.pqblackwell.com

Concept, design and text copyright © 2011 PQ Blackwell Limited
Book design by Cameron Gibb and Dayna Stanley
Research and image selection by Geoff Blackwell, Kelsen Butler, Lisette du Plessis and Jacqui Blanchard

All rights reserved. No part of this publication may be reproduced or transmitted in any form or by any means, electronic or mechanical, including photocopying, recording, or any information storage and retrieval systems without permission in writing from the publisher.

Printed by Everbest Printing International Limited